$15.45

Creative Caribbean Cooking & Menus

By
Master Chefs

Elsa Miller
Leonard 'Sonny' Henry

with
Special Barbecue Recipes

Kingston Publishers Limited

©T.E.P. Bahamas Co. Ltd.

First edition   1982
Reprinted   1984
Revised printing   1989
Reprinted   1991
Reprinted   1995

All rights reserved. No part of this book may be reproduced, stored in a retrieval system, or transmitted in any form or by any means, electronic, mechanical, photocopying, recording, or otherwise, without prior permission of the Publishers.

ISBN 976-625-016-2

Published by Kingston Publishers Limited
1a Norwood Avenue, Kingston 5, Jamaica

Lithographed in Jamaica by Stephensons

CONTENTS

FOREWORD..............................IV
APPETIZERS AND HORS D'OEUVRES...... 1
SOUPS 6
FISH AND SHELLFISH....................11
POULTRY 18
MEATS.................................24
VEGETABLES 30
SALADS................................37
DRESSINGS AND SAUCES................43
BARBECUES 47
PICKLES AND PRESERVES 56
JELLIES AND JAMS 60
DESSERTS.............................63
CAKES AND BREADS...................70
BEVERAGES 77
MENUS................................80
GLOSSARY OF COOKING TERMS.........84
35 USEFUL COOKING AND
HOUSEHOLD HINTS.....................86
TABLE OF MEASUREMENTS AND
MISCELLANEOUS EQUIVALENTS 88
SOME SUBSTITUTIONS 88
QUANTITIES PER HEAD 89
USEFUL KITCHEN EQUIPMENT 89
INDEX 90

Foreword

This is a cookbook devoted to people who delight in tasty, spicy food. The special sections on Barbecues and Menus will be a helpful aid to those who enjoy entertaining. The index also makes the book a useful reference for those interested in serious cuisine.

The recipes in the book reflect to a large extent the cultural heritage of the people in Jamaica: thus you will find recipes that reflect the Indian, African, European and both North and Latin American aspects of its culinary character following the Jamaican motto "Out Of May One People." Many of the dishes have been adapted to make use of the food we grow, such as ackee, plantain, coconut, paw-paw, mango, cassava and many others, which are considered exotic in other parts of the world.

For our foreign visitors who wish to prepare at home some of the dishes they may have tasted in restaurants or hotels, this book will be a handy guide. In many cases they will be able to find the ingredients they need in their local markets or West Indian communities.

For those who live here, may this book encourage a new and happy familiarity with foods we grow.

The Publishers

Appetizers & Hors d'oeuvres

OYSTERS

The best way to eat fresh oysters is raw. Open, and lay on a bed of crushed ice. Dress with lime juice. Brown bread and butter is usually served.

CURRIED CODFISH

½ lb. salt codfish
2 tablespoons minced onion
1 tablespoon curry powder

1 teaspoon lime juice
* flour
* oil

Wash fish, and cut into strips. Flour lightly and fry in bubbling oil. Take out the fish. Fry onion in the pan. Sprinkle with curry powder and moisten with lime juice. Allow to simmer, then add slices of fish and heat through. Serve on toast.

EGG PLANT ELEGANTE
(garden egg)

1 peeled egg plant
2 boiled crushed potatoes
* salt, pepper, flour, oil

* chopped garlic (1 clove)
* vinegar and oil

Slice garden egg lengthwise into fingers. Season with salt and pepper and roll in flour. Drop into deep hot oil and fry until crisp.

Combine crushed potatoes, garlic and enough vinegar and oil to make a paste of dipping consistency. Place in a bowl and use fried egg plant fingers as scoops.

GRAPEFRUIT WITH SHRIMP AND SOUR CREAM

½ grapefruit per person
6 shrimps, cooked and cleaned per person

1 cup sour cream
1 tablespoon mayonnaise

Cut grapefruit in half. Core and remove pulp. Discard seeds.
Fill with cooked shrimps, marinated in sour cream and mayonnaise and mixed with grapefruit pulp.

PINEAPPLE APPETIZER

* pieces of fresh pineapple
* cream cheese

* chopped cashew nuts

Dip pieces of pineapple in cheese and roll in cashews. Serve on toothpicks.

COCONUT CHIPS

1 dry coconut

Remove meat from shell. Cut meat into thin strips and arrange in a shallow pan. Sprinkle with salt and toast in a slow oven. Stir occasionally.

FRIED PLANTAIN CHIPS

1 green plantain

* oil

Peel plantain and cut into 1/6" thick slices. Fry in hot oil. Drain on paper towel. Sprinkle with salt to serve.

PORK RIND (SKIN)

* whatever quantity desired
2-3 tablespoon oil

* salt

Cut rind (skin) into small pieces and fry until crisp in oil. Sprinkle with salt.

COCO FRITTERS

2 cocos	* chopped escallion, salt pepper
1 tablespoon flour	1 egg
1 teaspoon baking powder	* oil

Wash and peel cocos. Grate and mix with other ingredients. Drop by spoonfuls into hot oil. When golden brown, remove and drain.

ACKEE WITH CHEESE

3 cups cooked ackees, crushed	1 tablespoon each butter, salt, pepper
2 cups mild grated cheese	

Mix all together, heat through and serve on toast.

NASSAU CAKE

4 tomatoes	1 tablespoon chopped onion
2 sweet peppers	* oil, salt, pepper
3 green or black olives	1 french type loaf of bread

Make this the day before it is to be used.

Chop tomatoes, peppers and olives. Add onion and seasoning. Cut bread in half lengthwise. Remove the crumbs and mix them into the tomato mixture, kneading it with a little oil, salt and pepper.

Fill the bread halves, and press together. Wrap in foil and refrigerate. Cut in slices to serve.

PEPPER SHRIMPS

1 pint of shrimps	½ sliced onion
* white vinegar, water	* salt and pimento grains
* sliced hot pepper (remove the seeds)	

Cover shrimps with salted water and boil until tender. Cool, peel and clean them. Meanwhile mix vinegar, peppers, onions and pimento grains. Bring to a boil Pour over shrimps and store in a covered jar for 12 hours before serving.

RIO COBRE MUD

1 chopped onion
1 tablespoon butter
1 tin red pea soup
3 tablespoons grated cheese
* creole sauce to taste
* a drop of hot sauce

Fry onion in butter. Add red pea soup and cheese. Stir over a low flame until cheese is melted.
Add sauces to taste and serve hot on slices of toast.

SEA URCHIN (Sea Eggs)

3 doz. sea eggs (not the black spiny type)

Wash well, open and remove the coral. This can be mixed with a white sauce and served on toast.
Sea eggs are considered a delicacy in many countries. The coral is scraped out and eaten raw with a squeeze of lemon or lime.

WATER MELON MARBLES

1 water melon
¼ pint rum
2 oranges
2 tablespoons sugar
* cherries

Cut the melon in half lengthwise. Remove the seeds, then with a ball-scoop remove the flesh of the melon. The shell can be kept to be a serving dish if wished.
Place the melon balls in a bowl. Mix the rum, orange juice and sugar together and pour over the melon balls. Refrigerate for at least one hour.
To serve, place a cocktail stick in each ball and pile up on a bed of cracked ice in the melon shell.

SEASONED BREADFRUIT CHIPS WITH AVOCADO CREAM CHEESE DIP

Breadfruit Chips
1   breadfruit
*   salt
*   black pepper
*   onion salt
*   garlic powder
*   oil

Peel breadfruit, cut into sections and remove the heart. Cut into slices and place in salted water for half an hour or more. Dry the slices and fry in hot fat until golden. Drain on paper towels. Meanwhile, mix the salt and seasonings together and sprinkle over the chips just before serving.

Avocado Cream Cheese Dip
1   medium avocado pear
6   ozs. cream cheese
½   teaspoon minced onion
1   tablespoon lemon or lime juice
2   tablespoons milk
*   salt

Halve avocado lengthwise and remove seed. Scoop out the pulp. The shell can be saved to be used as a container for serving, otherwise discard. Mash the pulp with cream cheese and other ingredients. Serve piled in a small dish or the shell, surrounded by breadfruit chips.

STAMP AND GO

The recipe for codfish fritters on page 11 makes a very popular cocktail snack when the fritters are made small and kept crisp. They can be served with the Avocado Dip above or with a fish-flavoured dip.

TASTY JERK PORK BITES

1 lb. jerk pork
1 small onion
1 small country pepper
½ teaspoon powdered ginger
2 teaspoons Pickapeppa sauce
2 ozs. rum

Cut jerk pork into small pieces and place in blender. Remove seeds from country pepper and place in blender with other ingredients. Blend until smooth. Chill.
Serve on small, bite-size crackers.

Soups

BAHAMIAN CONCH SOUP

1 cup of cooked and chopped conch meat which has been boiled in 1 qrt. of water
½ lb. diced tomatoes
½ lb. sliced onions
2 tablespoons oil
* herbs, garlic, salt to taste
* sherry optional

Heat oil and fry onions, tomatoes, and seasonings. Add these ingredients to conch meat and liquid. Cook about 20 minutes.

1 teaspoon sherry is often added to this. Only the meat of the young queen conch must be used.

CHOCHO PUREE

4 chochos peeled and diced
1 cup milk
* butter, herbs, salt, nutmeg to taste

Boil chocho until tender. Pour into blender with herbs and milk and blend until smooth. Reheat to serve with a dab of butter and pinch of nutmeg.

COCO SOUP

4 cocos
1 lb. soup meat
2 qrts. water
2 slices of bacon
1 tablespoon butter

Chop up cocos and place in a pot with water and soup meat and bacon. Boil until cocos are soft and meat is cooked.

Remove meat, put cocos and liquid through a blender or sieve.

Season to taste. Add the meat and a dab of margarine. Reheat to serve.

COCKEREL SOUP

4 lb. cockerel (a young cock)
2 qrts. water
2 sliced carrots
2 sliced potatoes
* onion, thyme, salt and a hot pepper

Boil the cockerel in water. When tender, strain and skim. Add vegetables, seasonings, and strips of the meat to the liquid.

Boil until vegetables are tender. Water may be added if it has boiled away.

Remove the hot pepper without breaking it in the cooking liquid.

COLD THICK CUCUMBER SOUP

½ cup diced cucumber
¾ cup diced cooked chicken
1 cup diced and cooked lobster meat
¼ cup chopped onion
1 cup milk
2 tablespoons sour cream
* salt, pepper, parsley

Mix the milk into the sour cream and thin down. Add all other ingredients. Chill for 2 hours before serving.

BEET SOUP

8 large cooked and peeled beets
1 lb. soup meat cut into cubes
3 diced tomatoes
2 qrts. water
1 cup shredded cabbage
* salt, pepper
* sour cream

Combine meat, tomatoes and water in a saucepan. Bring to a boil. Skim and cook for about an hour.

Add the cabbage, salt, and pepper. Cook for 30 minutes.

Grate the beetroots and add to the soup with salt and pepper. Cook for 15 minutes.

Serve very hot, with a spoonful of sour cream and a few pieces of the meat in each soup bowl.

COW HEEL SOUP

1 pr. cow heels
6 cups water
1 chopped onion
1 diced chocho
1 diced carrot
1 chopped coco
1 hot pepper
2 teaspoons salt
* squeeze of lime juice
* parsley

Wash cow heels in lime juice. Cut up and boil in salted water. Skim frequently. Cook 2–3 hours over low heat.

Add vegetables and seasonings. Boil until vegetables are tender. Serve with chopped parsley.

FISH CHOWDER

- 2 lbs. of any type of white fish meat
- 1 qrt. water
- 1 minced onion
- 2 diced carrots
- 1 diced potato
- 2 diced tomatoes
- * salt and pepper to taste
- * sherry, optional

Boil fish in water until tender. Remove all bones and strain the liquid. Stir diced vegetables into fish stock with seasonings. When cooked add some flaked fish meat and sherry to taste.

JAMAICA FISH TEA

- 3 lbs. of fish cut into pieces
- 6 cups water
- 2 chopped onions
- 2 chopped tomatoes
- 1 hot pepper
- 1 tsp. thyme
- * squeeze of lime juice

Place all ingredients in a pot with water. Bring to a boil and simmer gently for about an hour.
Strain off liquid and serve with chopped parsley.

GOAT HEAD SOUP (surya)— India

- 1 goat head
- 1 lb. pumpkin
- 1 lb. carrots
- 1 chocho
- 6 green bananas
- 1 lb. yellow yam
- 12 small dumplings
- 1 chopped onion
- * herbs, salt, pepper and a small piece of crushed ginger root
- 3 qrts. water

Prepare and clean goat's head. Put to boil in a large soup pot with water. Skim. When meat is tender, remove bones and put flesh back into liquid. Keep boiling.
Prepare and add the vegetables, seasoning and peppers. Soup must be of thick consistency. Serves 6.

GUNGU OR COW PEA SOUP

- 1 pint of peas (soaked overnight)
- 2 qrts. water
- 1 lb. soup meat
- 1 sliced coco
- 1 chopped onion
- * thyme, salt, pepper

Boil peas with soup meat in water until tender. Remove the meat and put peas through a colander, rub out and discard skin.
Place liquid on stove with seasonings and coco. Add more water if necessary.
When coco is cooked and dissolved, the soup is ready. Bits of the boiled meat can be added.

PAW PAW (PAPAYA) SOUP — Nigeria

- 2 tablespoons butter
- 1 sliced onion
- 1 paw paw peeled, seeded and sliced — use a fruit which is past the green stage but not yet ripe
- 3 cups water
- * a sprig of parsley
- * salt, pepper and a dash of nutmeg
- 3 cups milk
- 1 tablespoon cornstarch

Melt butter and fry onions. Add the paw paw, water, parsley, salt and pepper. Cover and boil over a low heat for about one hour, or until paw paw is tender enough to force through a sieve.

Return to saucepan and add nutmeg. Mix cornstarch into milk until smooth, and add to the paw paw mixture. Stir, constantly.

Cook for 10 minutes more over low heat, but do not allow to boil.

PEPPER POT

- 2 lbs. of chopped callaloo or spinach
- 2 qrts. water
- 1 lb. soup meat
- 2 slices bacon or a pig's tail
- 1 lb. pre-cooked shrimp
- 1 doz. okras sliced
- 1 minced onion
- 1 diced coco
- * salt, pepper, herbs, hot pepper to taste

Place meat and bacon in a soup pot with water. Boil until meat is tender.

Add callaloo, okras, coco and seasonings. Simmer until soup has thickened.

Remove hot pepper and meat (or may be left in if desired). Small flour dumplings (optional) and the shrimps are added. Simmer for 15 minutes longer.

PUMPKIN SOUP

- 2 lbs. pumpkin
- 2 qrts. water
- 1 lb. soup meat
- * a small piece of salt pork
- 3 pieces chopped escallion
- 1 chopped coco
- * thyme, salt, hot pepper

Place meat and salt pork in water and boil until meat is tender. Remove the meats.

Add peeled diced pumpkin, seasonings and chopped coco. Boil until vegetables are dissolved.

Taste for seasoning. Press through a colander and heat to serve.

SEA WEED SOUP (Irish Moss)

- 2 cups chicken broth
- 1 chopped onion
- 1 beaten egg
- 1 cup washed sea weed
- * salt and pepper

Mix chicken broth, onion, sea weed and seasonings. Bring to a boil and simmer for about 20 minutes.

Remove the sea weed and add the beaten egg to the broth when it is cool. Reheat to serve, but do not boil.

RED PEA SOUP

1 pint of red peas (soak overnight)
2 qrts. water
1 lb. soup meat
¼ lb. of pig's tail

1 sliced coco
1 minced onion
* salt, thyme, hot pepper to taste

Place peas and meats in water. Boil until peas are almost tender. Add coco and seasonings. When peas and coco are cooked, remove the meats.

Soup may be served with whole peas, or, put through a colander and discard skins. Small dumplings are usually added to this soup.

TRIPE SOUP

4 lbs. tripe
½ cup vinegar
1 pair pig's trotters
2 chopped onions

2 diced potatoes
2 cups diced chochos
* salt and pepper
4 qrts. water

Soak tripe and trotters in vinegar with water to cover for 2 hours. Drain and rinse.

Place tripe, trotters and 4 qrts. of water into a pot. Bring to a boil and skim. Cook over a low heat for about 3 hours.

Strain off the liquid. Cut tripe into small pieces and set aside. Discard trotters. Using about 6 cups of the liquid, add seasonings and vegetables. Cook for about ½ hour.

Add the tripe and simmer for a further ten minutes. Correct seasoning. This is a thick soup.

CLEAR TURTLE SOUP

3 lbs. of turtle meat
3 qrts. of water
3 diced carrots
2 diced onions

* salt — thyme — 6 pimento grains
* lime peel — a pinch of sage
* sherry to taste

Set all ingredients except lime peel and sage to boil for about 3 hours. One hour before straining, add a piece of lime peel, and some sage. Strain through a fine sieve.

Add some sherry and pieces of the turtle meat when serving.

THICK TURTLE SOUP

This is prepared in the same way as Clear Turtle Soup, except that it is thickened with 1 oz. of cornflour mixed with a little liquid for every qrt. of the soup.

Fish & Shellfish

STUFFED CALAPEEVA
(found in Jamaican rivers)

6 calapeeva	2 sliced onions
1 cup breadcrumbs	1 tablespoon rum
* parsley, salt, pepper to taste	1 tablespoon oil
1 dessertspoon butter	

Wash and clean fish with lime juice. Make a stuffing of breadcrumbs, parsley, salt and pepper, moistened with a little melted butter.

Stuff the fish and place on a bed of sliced onions, which have been slightly sauteed in hot oil. Add 1 tablespoon rum and cover with some breadcrumbs. Bake in a moderate oven until fish are tender.

STAMP AND GO (CODFISH FRITTERS)

¼ lb. salted codfish	1 minced onion
* lime juice	1 diced tomato
¼ lb. flour	¼ teaspoon hot pepper sauce
* water	

Wash codfish with lime juice, dry, and mince with onions and tomatoes. Add the flour and hot sauce with a little water to make a batter.

Heat some oil in a skillet. Drop the mixture by spoonfuls into the skillet and press down so that fritters are quite thin.

Fry on both sides until golden brown and crisp. Drain on paper towel and serve warm.

BANANA KING FISH WITH MUSTARD SAUCE

4 king fish steaks	* salt
2 ripe bananas	* pepper
4 slices Cheddar cheese	* butter

Season the fish steaks with salt and pepper. Fry gently in butter.

Place the steaks in a heat-proof dish. Cover each steak with slices of ripe banana and top with a slice of cheddar cheese. Broil until the cheese is melted and the banana heated through. Serve with mustard sauce.

Mustard Sauce

4 tablespoons mayonnaise	1 teaspoon lime juice
4 tablespoons vinegar	3 teaspoons dry mustard
4 tablespoons salad oil	* salt and pepper to taste

Mix all ingredients until smooth.

CODFISH BALLS

1 lb. codfish	* black pepper
1 lb. fresh pumpkin	* salt
1 tablespoon butter, softened	2 cups fresh breadcrumbs
2 eggs	* oil

Soak fish overnight. Discard water and cover with cold water. Bring to a boil and cook until tender. Skin, bone and flake finely.

Cook the pumpkin until tender. Mash thoroughly then beat in the softened butter, 2 lightly beaten eggs and pepper. Add salt to taste. The mixture should be firm enough to hold its shape. If not, beat in breadcrumbs as needed.

Shape the mixture into balls, dipping each in the breadcrumbs. Fry for about 3 to 4 minutes, turning regularly. When golden brown, drain on paper towels. Serve warm. A tomato sauce goes well with this dish.

BAKED BLACK CRABS

6 Black Crabs, boiled	1 teaspoon vinegar
1 oz. butter, softened	* salt
½ teaspoon black pepper	* breadcrumbs
1 tablespoon chopped onion	* butter
1 country pepper, finely chopped	

Clean the crabs and pick out all the meat, including the claws and smaller bones. Save four shells.

Mix the crab meat with the butter, onion, pepper, salt and vinegar. The mixture should be moist but not soggy.

Wash the shells well and wipe with a little oil. Fill each with the crab mixture, top with the breadcrumbs and dot with butter. Bake in a hot oven until the crumbs are brown.

BAHAMIAN CONCH FRITTERS

- 1 lb. raw minced conch meat
- 1 minced onion
- 4 ozs. flour
- 1 egg
- * salt, pepper
- 2 tablespoons dry breadcrumbs
- * milk and fat as needed

Mix conch meat, onion, flour, egg and seasoning together and moisten with a little milk. Shape into flat fritters. Dip in breadcrumbs and fry quickly in hot oil.

CODFISH TWICE LAID

- 1 lb. salt fish
- 1 lb. potatoes, boiled & sliced
- 1 sliced onion
- 2 tablespoons margarine or butter
- * breadcrumbs
- * pepper to taste

Soak fish overnight. Discard water and cover with cold water. Bring to a boil and cook until tender. Skin, bone and flake.

Fry onion lightly and add to the fish. In a casserole place alternate layers of potatoes with fish-onion mixture. Dot layers with butter and cover with breadcrumbs before baking until golden brown in a moderate oven.

SALTFISH AND ACKEE

- 1 lb. codfish
- 12–14 ackees
- 2 ozs. fried bacon
- 4 ozs. margarine
- 2 tablespoons margarine or butter
- * breadcrumbs
- * pepper to taste

Soak fish overnight and discard the water. Cover with cold water and boil until tender. Skin, bone and flake, and set aside.

Prepare ackees and boil quickly. In a separate pan, melt margarine, stir in onions tomatoes and pepper. Simmer a few minutes, then add the fish and ackees. Heat through to serve.

CRAB FRITTERS

- ½ lb. cooked crab meat (use local black crabs)
- 2 tablespoons oil
- 1 tablespoon chopped onion
- 3 eggs
- 1 tablespoon minced parsley
- * breadcrumbs, salt, pepper to taste

Add onion, seasoning and beaten egg to crab meat. Add enough breadcrumbs to bind mixture. Shape into fritters and fry lightly.

ESCOVEITCH OF FISH (GROUPER)

* small fish or slices of king fish
* oil
1 cup vinegar
2 sliced onions
2 tablespoons water
1 chopped hot pepper
* a pimento leaf and a pinch of salt

Fry fish in hot oil and set aside. Mix remaining ingredients together and bring to a boil. Simmer 20 minutes.
Lay fish in a shallow dish. Cover with hot vinegar sauce and marinate for about 12 hours before serving.
(In Mexico the fish is not cooked, it is marinated and eaten raw.)

FISH KEDGEREE

1 cup cooked rice
* curry powder
* mushrooms, optional
* lime rind
1 cup cooked fish, tuna, salmon or codfish
* salt
3 hard-boiled eggs

Toss together cooked rice and flaked, cooked fish. Add a pinch of curry powder and some chopped mushrooms if available, a pinch of salt and a sprinkle of lime rind.
Pack into a mould and bake for 30 minutes. Serve with chopped hard boiled eggs.

JAMAICA FISH PIE

2 cups cooked flaked fish
1 cup white sauce (see page 43)
1 cup cooked peeled shrimps
* salt, pepper, chopped parsley
1 cup cooked, mashed potatoes
1 cup flour
* pinch of salt
1 beaten egg

Mix together fish, white sauce, shrimp, seasonings and parsley and place in a deep pie dish.
Mix remaining ingredients to form a dough. Roll out on a floured board and cut to cover pie.
Place dough over fish mixture and prick top with a fork. Bake in a moderate oven about 30 minutes or till crust is brown.

BAKED GRUNTS

6 grunts
* juice of 2 limes
* water, hot pepper, salt
3 tablespoons butter
* avocado slices

Clean grunts, place in a greased dish and add lime juice and water to cover. Add salt and pieces of hot pepper.
Cover and bake in a $350°$ oven for about 20 minutes. Spread melted butter over them and serve with avocado slices.

KING FISH IN COCONUT CREAM

2 lbs. fish steaks
3 ozs. butter or margarine
1 cup coconut cream

* salt, pepper
* lime slices

Heat butter and fry steaks until brown on both sides.
To make coconut cream, grate a coconut, add water, squeeze and strain out cream. Discard pulp.
Add to fish steaks with salt and pepper.
Simmer for about 3 minutes. Garnish with lime slices.

KING FISH FILLETS

4 fillets of king fish
1 glass white wine
1 cup cooked and peeled shrimps
1 cup white sauce
1 egg

* a pinch of salt and pepper
* a squeeze of lime juice
2 tablespoons tomato sauce
1 cup breadcrumbs
2-3 tablespoons margarine or oil

Soak fillets in white wine, salt, pepper, and lime juice for 1 hour. Pat dry.
Make 1 cup of white sauce and add the cooked shrimps. When this is cool, spoon some of the mixture onto each fish and roll up.
Dip in breadcrumbs, then into beaten egg and again in crumbs. Fry in hot oil. Serve with tomato sauce.

LOBSTER CREOLE

2 lbs. cooked and shredded lobster meat
2 chopped onions
2 chopped sweet peppers

3 diced tomatoes
2 tablespoons rum or sherry
4 tablespoons oil
* salt, pepper, to taste

Fry onion and peppers until tender. Stir in salt and pepper. Add tomatoes and simmer gently. Add lobster meat with rum or sherry.
Continue to simmer gently for about 10 minutes. Serve with plain boiled rice.

MACKEREL ALOHA

1 tin drained mackerel
½ cup diced pineapple
2 tablespoons chopped peanuts

¼ cup mayonnaise
1 tablespoon lime juice

Break up mackerel. Combine with remaining ingredients and toss.
Serve in shells or lettuce cups.
Sardines can also be served in this manner.

OCTOPUS (called by local fishermen "Sea Puss")

1 small octopus
3 tablespoons butter
* salted water to cover

Cut octopus into small pieces and place in a pot of salted water. Bring to a boil and cook until octopus is tender. Drain, dry and fry in butter. Serve with one of the following sauces.

PIQUANT SAUCE

1 tablespoon oil
2 tablespoons vinegar
½ chopped onion
* pinch salt and pepper

Mix all ingredients together.

CHEESE SAUCE

6 tablespoons flour
6 tablespoons margarine
2 cups milk
1 cup grated cheese
* salt to taste

Melt margarine and blend in flour and milk. Stir all the time until thick. Add cheese and salt. Heat until cheese is melted.

SHRIMP WITH PINEAPPLE

24 large shrimp, cleaned, peeled and cooked
1 tablespoon cornflour
½ pint pineapple juice
2 tablespoons soya sauce
1 tablespoon honey
1 tablespoon vinegar
¼ teaspoon ginger powder
1 small tin of pineapple chunks

Blend cornflour with a little of the pineapple juice. Combine with remaining juice, soya sauce, honey, vinegar and ginger. Cook over a low heat, stirring until thickened.

Thread shrimps and pineapple chunks alternately on to skewers and dip into sauce. Grill until slightly golden in colour.

BAKED SPICY SNOOK
(found in Jamaican rivers)

3 lbs. snook (prepared)
1 tablespoon salt
¼ teaspoon pepper
½ teaspoon nutmeg

1 tablespoon onion
½ cup melted butter
¼ cup soya sauce
2 tablespoons lime juice

Mix salt, pepper, nutmeg, onion and rub into the fish, inside and outside.
Wrap in foil and bake about 20 minutes in a moderate oven.
Whilst fish is baking combine butter, lime juice and soya sauce. At the end of 20 minutes pour this sauce over the fish.
Cover and bake 20 minutes longer.

SOLOMON GUNDY

½ lb. pickled herring
½ lb. pickled shad
1/3 cup vinegar
1 tablespoon oil

1 tablespoon chopped onion
* a few pimento grains
* a few drops of hot pepper sauce

Soak the fish for 3 hours in water to cover. Pour off the water and scald the fish with boiling water. Remove the skin, let cool, and shred flesh.
Boil vinegar with onion and pimento grains. Add oil and pour over fish.
Pack into jars, cover and keep in the refrigerator.

RED STRIPE BATTER FOR FISH

¼ cup cornstarch
¾ cup flour
¼ cup beer (Red Stripe)

2 egg whites
¼ cup margarine or oil
* salt to taste

Any type of fish may be used.
Mix cornstarch and flour and salt. Add beer and beat until smooth. Beat egg whites and fold into batter.
Dip slices of fish or whole small fish into this batter and fry in bubbling fat.

Poultry

CHICKEN BAHAMAS

- 1 3 lb. chicken
- 2 cups cooked rice or spaghetti
- 3 ozs. cashew nuts
- * hot pepper sauce to taste
- * salt
- 2 chopped onions

Boil a chicken in the usual way. Reserve stock. Cut chicken into pieces and arrange on a bed of rice, or spaghetti. Prepare a sauce by pounding cashew nuts with some hot pepper sauce and a pinch of salt.

Fry two onoins and add to nut mixture, with some of the chicken stock. Pour over the chicken.

DRUNK CHICKEN

- 2 lbs. chicken cut in pieces
- 2 qrts. water
- 1 teaspoon salt
- * sherry or rum or white wine

Heat to boiling 2 qrts. of water, salt and chicken; Cover and simmer for about 15 minutes.

Place chicken in a bowl or jar and cover completely with liquor. Keep refrigerated for 1 week. Serve cold.

CHICKEN WITH LIME AND OLIVES

- 2½ lbs. chicken
- ¼ cup oil
- 1½ cups minced onions
- ½ teaspoon powdered ginger
- 1½ cups water
- 1 tablespoon lime juice
- 2 doz. small pitted olives
- * salt, pepper

Cut chicken into pieces and brown on all sides in oil. Remove chicken and fry onions.
Stir in ginger, salt and pepper and simmer 2 minutes. Add water, lime juice and chicken pieces. Simmer for 30 minutes. Add olives a few minutes before serving.

TROPICAL CHICKEN

4 young coconuts
1 small chicken
2 cups chicken broth
1 cup rice
1 cup chopped pineapple

1 diced onion
½ cup corn kernels
3 tablespoons curry powder
* salt, pepper

Slice off top of coconuts and take a thin slice off the bottoms also, so that the coconut will stand upright. Pour off water and reserve.

Steam chicken in coconut water. When tender, remove, cool and shred the meat.

Steam rice in 2 cups of broth (adding water if needed). Mix in pineapple, onions, corn and curry powder. Correct seasoning.

Stuff coconuts with this mixture, placing alternate layers with the shredded chicken. Replace tops on coconut and sit in a shallow pan of water. Bake in a moderate oven for one hour. If water in pan evaporates add more.

A DIFFERENT STUFFING FOR ROASTED CHICKEN

1 cup cooked rice
½ cup raisins
¼ cup finely chopped onions
* chopped parsley

* diced cooked chicken liver
2 ozs. butter
1 egg

Mash the chicken livers and mix all ingredients together, working the butter well into mixture. Add the beaten egg last to bind.

GUINEA HEN AFRICAN STYLE

½ lb. butter or margarine
2 small guinea hens cut into pieces
1 minced onion
1 tablespoon flour
1 cup water

3 chopped tomatoes
3 sweet potatoes, cubed
5 firm ripe plantains, sliced
* salt, pepper

Melt all but 3 tablespoons butter in a large pot or casserole. Add the guinea hen pieces, onions, some salt and pepper and saute in some of the butter. Sprinkle with flour and add water and tomatoes.

Cook over low heat for 25 minutes. Add sweet potato cubes and cook until tender. Correct seasoning.

Melt remaining butter and fry plantain slices. Skim all fat from gravy and serve plantain slices separately.

BRAISED GUINEA HEN

1 prepared guinea hen
* fat
1 lump of butter
1 lb. carrots

1 clove garlic
1 sliced onion
* parsley, thyme, salt, pepper to taste

Put butter inside guinea hen and brown in sizzling fat.

Clean and slice carrots lengthwise and add to pan with garlic, onion and herbs. Cover and cook about an hour depending on the age of the bird. Wine may be added to the sauce.

GUINEA FOWL STEW

1 guinea fowl
4 onions
2 tomatoes
2 hard boiled eggs
2 cups crushed peanuts

1 cup water
2 cloves garlic
½ teaspoon salt
* oil
* boiled white rice

Put peanuts into 1 cup water and boil for 12 minutes until the peanut oil shows on the side of the pot.

Cut up guinea fowl and saute in oil. Add diced tomatoes, onions and garlic. Finally, add all the peanuts and seasoning. Mix well and fry for 5 minutes.

Empty into a pot adding more water if needed and stew until flesh is tender.

When cooked, float halved hard boiled eggs on the top and serve with boiled white rice.

PIGEONS WITH CABBAGE

2 pigeons
1 small cabbage
1 onion
2 pieces bacon
½ cup water

* juice of 1 lime
½ cup raisins
* a pinch of salt
* sugar and pepper to taste

Cut the birds in half down the backbone. Melt fat from bacon and fry the birds in this. Remove birds.

Slice onion and saute in the same pan. Add sugar and raisins. Shred cabbage and add to the pan. Stir to coat.

Heat water and lime juice and add to pan with a sprinkle of salt.

Place the pieces of pigeons on top of the cabbage. Cover and simmer for about 1 hour. Correct seasoning.

PIGEON PIE

3 pigeons cut into pieces
* salt and pepper
3 tablespoons oil

* diced ham
2 cups chicken broth

Season pigeons with salt and pepper and fry in oil. Add diced ham and stock. Place in a deep pie dish and cover with crust. Bake in 350° oven 30 minutes or till crust is lightly browned.

PIE CRUST

1 cup flour
4 ozs. butter, margarine or shortening

2-3 tablespoons cold water
* pinch of salt

Sift together flour and salt. Mix fat into flour by using 2 knives and "cutting" in the fat till it is pea-sized and coated with flour. Sprinkle water over flour using a minimum amount to moisten mixture. Shape mixture into a mound and roll out. Cut to fit dish.

PIGEONS WITH PINEAPPLE

½ of a ripe pineapple
4 squabs (young pigeons)
¼ cup butter
¼ cup paté

4 tablespoons brandy or rum if preferred
* salt, pepper to taste
½ cup pineapple juice

Peel, slice and dice pineapple. Wash and dry squabs. Into each body cavity put 1 tablespoon pate and a piece of pineapple. Close cavity and rub squabs with salt and pepper.
Melt ½ of the butter in a heavy casserole and brown the squabs. Do not prick the skins.
Flame with 1 tablespoon brandy or rum (heat, ignite and pour over squabs). Pour in the remaining butter, and roast squabs in 350° oven uncovered, basting often, for about 45 minutes.
While squabs are roasting, poach slices of pineapple in the rest of liquor for 10 minutes. Arrange slices on the squabs to serve.

BALDPATE SPATCHCOCK

3 baldpate doves
2 tablespoons melted butter
1 teaspoon salt

1 teaspoon pepper
* juice of a lime
* fat for basting

Prepare doves, wash with lime juice and season. Split through the backbone and flatten the birds. Wipe dry.
Bake in hot oven basting frequently for about 15 minutes.
Remove from the oven, place under a grill, dribble melted butter over the birds and grill on both sides.

WHITE WING OR ANY OTHER DOVE WITH CREAM

4 doves	¼ pint cream (or evaporated milk)
4 slices bacon	* a few black olives
4 tablespoons butter	* salt and pepper to taste

Cover the breast of each bird with a slice of bacon and season. Place 1 tablespoon butter inside each bird.

Roast in a hot 400-450° oven for 30 minutes. Remove birds, drain off surplus fat and add cream to the pan.

Simmer slowly and season to taste. Add olives, and pour over the birds.

BRAISED DUCKLING

1 3½–4 lb. duckling	1 cup chicken stock
4 ozs. butter	½ lb. young sliced turnips
2 onions	2 ozs. butter
2 carrots	* salt, pepper to taste
¼ cup brandy or wine	

Brown duck on all sides in a casserole. Put in the onions and sliced carrots, browning them also.

Pour in the liquor and all the stock with salt and pepper. Place in a moderate oven 350° and baste frequently.

When duck is ready, keep it warm. Strain the liquid, remove vegetables and reduce the sauce.

Serve with the young turnips which have been cooked whilst duck was braising. Blanch the turnips first, then saute in butter.

SALMI OF DUCK

1 duck	1½ pints chicken stock (chicken cubes melted in water)
2 ozs. butter	* salt, pepper
1 oz. flour	* brandy or wine
1 onion, chopped	

Roast duck, cook till slightly underdone. Cut into neat joints.

Melt 1 oz. butter and fry onion. Add stock, simmer for 1 hour and strain. Melt remaining butter, stir in flour and add the stock. Season and simmer 15 minutes.

Add the pieces of duck and cook 20 minutes longer. Brandy or wine is usually added to taste.

DUCK AND PINEAPPLE

1   4lb. duck
1   tin pineapple slices
2   tablespoons oil
2   tablespoons soya sauce
1   tablespoon rum
½   cup water
2   tablespoons brown sugar
* a pinch of salt

Clean and roast the duck. Cool, remove bones and slice. Drain pineapple slices and dice. Place duck and pineapple in alternate layers in a casserole. Add the pineapple juice mixed with oil, soya sauce, rum, water, sugar and salt.
Bake in moderate oven for 1 hour. Serve with rice and green salad.

TEAL WITH ORANGE SAUCE

* teal (wild duck)
* salt and pepper
* oil

Prepare and season birds. Roast till done, in a moderate oven, basting with cooking fats and adding a little oil if necessary.

SAUCE

* juice of 2 oranges
* 2 cloves
1   dessertspoon cornstarch
1   tablespoon rum
* orange segments

Mix juice with cloves and thicken with cornstarch moistened first in some of the juice. Add rum and orange juice to liquid and boil very slowly to thicken in a double boiler. Serve over teal.

Meats

BEEF CURRY WITH GREEN BANANAS

3 peeled green bananas cut in ¼" slices
1½ lbs. stewing beef
3 tablespoons oil
2 tablespoons curry powder
2 onions

1½ tablespoons flour
½ cup tomato ketchup
½ teaspoon salt
½ cup rum

Boil bananas in salted water for 20 minutes. Drain and reserve.
Cut beef into cubes and brown in oil. Transfer to a saucepan.
Add sliced onions. Stir in flour, salt and tomato ketchup and cook for 5 minutes. Cover with curry powder mixed in some water. Stir and simmer for 1½ hrs. Add rum and green banana slices. Heat through.

BEEF AND MANGO IN BEER

12 ozs. minced beef
1 cup Red Stripe Beer
1 cup water
½ cup mango chutney

* pinch of salt and onion powder
1 dessertspoon soya sauce
½ cup rice
1 cup green peas

Combine first six ingredients in a casserole and bake in oven for 1 hour at 350°. Add rice and cook for ½ hour. Just before serving add the peas.

SALTED BEEF AND BANANA CASSEROLE

¼ lb. diced, cooked, salted beef
2 eggs
1 cup grated cheese

½ cup milk
1 cup diced ripe bananas
* salt, pepper, marjoram

Beat eggs, stir in cheese, beef, milk, pepper, marjoram and bananas. Use very little salt, if any. Turn into a casserole and bake for about 40 minutes in a 350° oven.

DUMPERPUMPKIN

1 small pumpkin
2 cups prepared sweet and sour beef

½ cup seeded prunes

Wash pumpkin and place in a large pot. Cover with water and bring to a boil. When cooked, but not soft, remove, cut off the top and scoop out seeds and core.

Fill with sweet and sour beef mix and prunes. Refit top. Place pumpkin in a baking dish with water and bake for 30-40 minutes in a moderate oven — add more water if necessary.

SWEET AND SOUR BEEF FILLING

2 lbs. steak, cubed
* fat or oil
1 tablespoon sugar
1 cup water
3 tablespoons vinegar

1 teaspoon soya sauce
1 teaspoon tomato ketchup
* pinch of salt and ginger powder
1 dessertspoon cornstarch

Fry steak in oil and cook through. In a separate pot, bring next six ingredients to a boil and thicken with a little cornstarch blended in some water.

Pour over the cubed steak. Simmer for about ½ hour.

Fill pumpkin cavity and transfer to oven for 30 mins.

RUMP STEAK CASSEROLE

2 lbs. steak
¼ lb. margarine
1 dessertspoon sugar
1 cup vinegar
1 cup beef stock (tin of beef bouillon or consomme)

* salt, pepper, nutmeg and ginger to taste
1 teaspoon marjoram
* chopped tomatoes, optional

Cut steaks into cubes and marinate for 2 hours in sugar, vinegar, seasoning and herbs. Melt margarine and brown beef cubes. Moisten with some of the marinade.

Place meat in a casserole with 1 cup of beef stock. Cover and bake in a 350° oven until tender.

Skim off fat and add a few chopped tomatoes if desired.

POOR MAN'S FILLET

3 lbs. rib eye steak
2 tablespoons butter
* salt, pepper, garlic powder to taste
* bread slices

Cut the steak allowing one slice per person. Rub with salt, pepper and garlic. Brown steak slices in hot butter. Fry slices of bread in butter.

Slip a slice of steak onto each slice of bread and serve with sauce from fry pan. Takes about 3 minutes to prepare.

CURRIED GOAT OR RABBIT

1 lb. goat or rabbit
2 tablespoons curry powder
2 sliced onions
2 cups hot water
1 tablespoon lime juice
1 tablespoon butter
* salt, oil

Cut meat into bite-size pieces, season with curry powder and salt and set aside for about one hour. Brown in hot oil.

Add 2 cups of hot water and onions. Cook slowly until tender, stirring to prevent burning. Add more curry powder if needed, butter and lime juice. Cook for about 20 minutes longer.

Serve with plain boiled rice and side dishes of nuts, grated coconut, mango chutney, sliced onions soaked in hot sauce and slices of fried ripe plantain.

BONED STUFFED LEG OF KID

1 boned leg of goat kid
1 cup breadcrumbs
* milk
1 egg yolk
* chopped parsley
* salt and pepper

Season meat with salt and pepper. Moisten breadcrumbs with milk and press dry. Add egg yolk, chopped parsley, salt and pepper to make a stuffing for meat.

Fill, roll, and tie meat and bake for 1½ hours in a 350° oven. Serve with baby carrots and small boiled onions.

MUTTON STEW (In Jamaica goat meat is often referred to as mutton)

3 lbs. goat meat
1 teaspoon hot sauce
1 cup chopped onions
* oil, salt, flour
1 cup sliced carrots
1 cup chopped tomatoes
1 cup sliced potatoes
4 cups hot water
* some small flour dumplings

Dredge cubed meat with flour and salt and brown in hot oil. Add water and simmer until meat is tender.

Add sauce, onions, and vegetables. Cook until vegetables are ready. This process should take about 2 hours.

When all is ready add the dumplings which will cook very quickly. Add more liquid if necessary.

LIVER WITH SWEET PEPPERS

1 lb. liver sliced thin
4 sweet peppers
1 teaspoon lime juice
1 tablespoon rum
½ cup oil
* salt, pepper, a little flour

Prepare sweet peppers by coring and removing seeds. Wash and cut into strips.
Season liver with salt, pepper and lime juice. Dust with flour and saute quickly in hot oil.
Pour the rum over liver. Add the slices of pepper and cook gently for 15-20 minutes.

PORK CHOPS WITH GINGER ALE

4 chops
* fat, salt, pepper
* parsley
* ginger ale

Brown chops lightly in fat. Add seasoning. Place in individual squares of foil. Sprinkle liberally with ginger ale. Fold squares tightly. Place in a baking dish and bake in a 350° oven for about 1½ hours.

MARINATED PORK CHOPS

4 chops
* salt, pepper
* lime juice
* garlic powder

Sprinkle the chops with seasonings and lime juice and marinate for 2 hours. Grill the chops and serve with a green salad. Instead of a dressing pour the juices from the grilling pan.

PORK CHOPS WITH PINEAPPLE

4 chops
1 cup pineapple chunks
8 prunes or 1 cup raisins
1 teaspoon grated lime peel
* sprinkle of sugar and salt
* breadcrumbs
* a lump of butter
2 cups shredded cabbage
* salt
¼ cup vinegar
1 tablespoon water

Brown chops and sprinkle with salt. In a casserole, place the chops in layers with the pineapple, prunes, peel and sugar.
Cover with breadcrumbs and dot with butter. Bake in a slow oven 300° for 1½ hours.
Serve with shredded cabbage which has been sprinkled with salt and boiled in vinegar and water. When tender, strain and serve hot.

JERKED PORK SNACKS

1 3–4 lbs. boned leg of pork
   (cut into bite size pieces)
1 cup vinegar
* chopped hot pepper
* chopped onion and garlic

* crushed pimento leaves
* pimento grains, salt

Marinate the pieces of pork in the marinade for 4 days turning frequently. Keep covered in refrigerator.

Take out and wipe dry. Cook pork on a grid over burning coals to get a smokey flavour; however, it can also be baked crisp on a baking sheet in the oven.

RABBIT FRICASSEE

1 rabbit cut into pieces
2 tablespoons vinegar
* oil or fat
* salt and pepper
2 sliced onions

2 slices bacon
1 cup chicken broth
2 tablespoons raisins
1 dessertspoon grated chocolate
1 teaspoon sugar

Wash rabbit in vinegar. Pat dry and saute in fat with sliced onions, bacon and seasonings Add broth and simmer slowly until rabbit is tender.

Add the sugar, chocolate and raisins to finish cooking. Do not be afraid of the chocolate, it gives a surprisingly pleasant flavour to this dish.

BRAWN (made also with Rabbit using the whole animal)

1 pig's head
* water, pimento leaves
* few cloves

* lime to taste
* salt to taste

Scrape and clean the head and wash with lime juice. Cover with water, pimento leaves, salt and cloves. Boil until tender.

Cut into chunks discarding the bones. Add lime juice to the liquid and pour over the brawn in a casserole. Place in the refrigerator to congeal.

ROASTED RABBIT

1 rabbit (skin and clean)	* salt, pepper
* sage	1 cup breadcrumbs
1 tablespoon butter	* bacon drippings
¼ cup milk	

Stuff rabbit with breadcrumbs mixed with the given ingredients. Sew up cavity. Rub all over with bacon dripping. Roast 1–1½ hrs. in a 350° oven.

SOUSE (From Barbados)

½ pig's head	¼ pint beef stock
1 pig's tongue	1 sliced onion
2 pig's trotters	* hot peppers to taste
4 limes	* juice from 2 limes
1 tablespoon salt	

Scald and scrape meats and wash with lime juice. Tie all meats into a cloth with a sprinkle of salt. Place in a pot and cover with cold water. Boil up and simmer for about 2 hours.

Cool in the liquid. Remove meat, skin and slice the tongue. Cut up the trotters and slice the meat from head. Place in a deep casserole.

Bring remaining ingredients to a boil and pour over meats.

Cover and reheat to serve. Can be used hot or chilled.

TRIPE WINDSOR

2 lbs. tripe	1 chopped onion
1 qrt. water	4 chopped tomatoes
2 onions	1 tablespoon brandy
2 carrots	2 ozs. margarine
1 cup stock	* grated nutmeg
* salt, thyme, parsley to taste	* salt and pepper

Wash tripe with lime juice and put into a stew pot with the water. Simmer for 2 hours.

Add vegetables, herbs and salt and simmer until tripe is tender and the vegetables cooked. Remove tripe from the stock and cut into small pieces.

Mix tripe and vegetables with remaining ingredients in a covered casserole. Bake in a moderate oven for 35 minutes.

Vegetables

BEANS IN SOUR CREAM SAUCE

1 lb. green beans (string beans)
2 tablespoons butter
* salt

Boil beans uncovered, strain, melt butter, add beans and toss. Season with salt and pepper. Top with this sauce.

SAUCE

1 cup sour cream
¼ cup milk
* a few drops of lime juice,
* a pinch of garlic powder

Mix ingredients together and pour over beans.

BROAD BEAN CUTLETS

1 lb. broad beans (or sugar beans)
1 oz. margarine
2 eggs
1 teaspoon minced onion
1 teaspoon chopped parsley
6 ozs. crushed potatoes
* bread crumbs
* salt and pepper to taste

Cook beans in boiling water with salt and onions. Puree by rubbing through a sieve.
Add melted margarine, crushed potatoes, seasoning, and enough of the beaten eggs to bind into a paste. Add enough bread crumbs to shape into cutlets and coat with egg and more bread crumbs. Fry in deep hot fat. Drain and serve warm.

STUFFED BREADFRUIT

1 medium size breadfruit
1 tablespoon butter
¼ cup milk
1 small chopped onion
* a pinch of salt

Stuffed breadfruit is first roasted for an hour in the skin — roasted over charcoal is of course the best way, but it can be done over a gas burner.

When cooked, cut a circle in the top, scoop out heart and discard, then scoop out the flesh.

Crush this, cream with milk and butter and season with a little salt and onion. To this may be added minced beef, codfish and ackee, or left over stew etc.

Pack into the cavity, wrap with foil and put into the oven to warm through before serving.

BAKED CABBAGE

3 cups shredded cabbage
2 cups breadcrumbs
1 cup grated cheese
2 eggs
1 teaspoon salt
1 teaspoon prepared mustard
2 cups milk
1/8 teaspoon pepper

Cover cabbage with water, bring to a boil and drain. In a shallow 2 qrt. dish, arrange cabbage, breadcrumbs and cheese in layers.

Beat eggs with salt, pepper and mustard. Add milk and pour over the cabbage. Let stand for 15 minutes. Bake for 45 minutes in a 350° oven.

FRUITED CABBAGE

1½ lbs. shredded cabbage
2 ozs. raisins
2 diced onions
1 cup water
1 cup diced pineapple
* juice of 1 lime

Mix cabbage with fruit and onions. Add 1 cup water, lime juice and a pinch of salt. Cook for about 40 minutes or until liquid has evaporated.

CALLALOO BAKE

1 bunch callaloo cooked and diced
1 diced onion
2 slices bacon fried and diced
2 tablespoons grated cheese
¼ cup crushed potatoes
1 cup breadcrumbs

Mix first three ingredients in a casserole. Top with breadcrumbs, cheese and potatoes. Bake for about 35 minutes in a moderate oven.

FRUITY CALLALOO

1 bunch callaloo, chopped
1 cup grapefruit juice
* salt, pepper

Wash and prepare callaloo, add salt and pepper. Put into a pot with grapefruit juice. Cook quickly for 10 minutes. Drain, correct seasoning and serve.

CARROT AMBROSIA

12 carrots
2 tablespoons butter or margarine
2 tablespoons sugar
2 sliced oranges

Glaze 12 small carrots by melting the sugar and butter in a pan and turning the carrots, either sliced or whole, in the mixture over a moderate heat till golden brown.
Add 2 sliced oranges and reheat to serve.

MINT GLAZED CARROTS

12 small carrots (pre-cooked)
¼ cup butter
1 teaspoon mint sauce
¼ cup sugar

Simmer carrots in the butter. Add mint sauce and sugar. Cook until sugar has melted.

CAULIFLOWER CUSTARD

1 cauliflower
2 eggs
1 cup milk
* salt, nutmeg, garlic powder

Boil cauliflower in some salt and water. When cool, break off flowerets and put into a greased dish.
Beat 2 eggs with milk and garlic powder. Pour over cauliflower. Sprinkle with nutmeg. Bake until set.

CHOCHOS BAKED WITH CHEESE

3 chochos, boiled and sliced
½ cup grated cheese
* dabs of butter or margarine

Place chocho slices in a casserole, in alternate layers with grated cheese and dabs of butter, ending with cheese. Bake until cheese has melted and is crisp on top.

ACKEE SOUFFLE

1 dozen ackees	4 eggs, separated
3 tablespoons butter	1 oz. cheese, grated
3 tablespoons flour	* salt
1 cup milk	* pepper
	1 teaspoon Worcestershire sauce

Prepare ackees by discarding seeds and taking out pink skin. Wash in salt water. Boil quickly and crush.

In a heavy saucepan, melt the butter and stir in flour. Cook for one minute then add the milk gradually, stirring steadily. Continue cooking and stirring until the mixture thickens then add the salt, pepper and Worcestershire sauce. Remove from heat and allow to cool a little.

Stir in the grated cheese then beat in the egg yolks one by one. Add the crushed ackee and allow the mixture to cool to room temperature.

Preheat the oven to 375°. Butter a 2½ pint souffle dish or fireproof casserole.

Beat the egg whites until stiff. Mix one quarter of the whites into the ackee mixture, then fold in the rest. Pour into the prepared dish and bake in the middle of the oven for 30 minutes when the souffle should be well risen and firm. Serve immediately.

FRIED ACKEES

1 dozen ackees (or more)	* butter
salt water	

Prepare ackees by discarding seeds and taking out pink skin. Cover in salt water for five minutes. Drain.

Fry in hot butter. Drain on paper towels and serve.

This recipe can be used for tinned ackees.

BEETS WITH ORANGE SAUCE

6 beets (about 1½ lbs.)	¼ cup orange juice
2 tablespoons sugar	1 tablespoon lime juice
1 tablespoon cornstarch	½ teaspoonful grated orange rind
¼ teaspoon salt	1 tablespoon butter

Boil beets in salted water until tender. Drain, reserving the water. Peel the beets and dice.

Combine sugar, cornstarch and salt in the top of a double boiler. Gently stir in ¼ cup of liquid from the cooked beets and the orange juice. Cook over boiling water until thick and smooth, stirring constantly.

Remove from the heat. Stir in remaining ingredients. Add the diced beets and mix lightly. Keep warm over hot water until ready to serve.

STUFFED CHOCHO OR SQUASH

3 chochos or 1 small squash
9 tablespoons minced beef
6 tablespoons bread crumbs
1 tablespoon margarine

1 minced onion
* salt, pepper, oil
* grated cheese

Cut chochos or squash in half and boil until tender but firm. Scrape out the inside and dice, being careful not to break the skin. Saute onions and minced beef in oil and add diced chocho or squash. Fill shells, top with breadcrumbs and a sprinkle of cheese. Bake in 350° oven until brown on top.

CORN FRITTERS

1 tin corn kernels
1 cup milk
1 tablespoon flour

4 tablespoons margarine or butter
* pinch of salt

Make a batter of milk, flour and salt. Fold in whole corn kernels and drop by spoonfuls into bubbling butter or margarine. Fry on both sides.

EGG PLANT (Garden Egg) with CHEESE AND TOMATOES

2 large eggplants
2 sliced onions
2 sliced tomatoes
1 cup grated cheese

1½ cups water
2 tablespoons oil
* salt, pepper and mixed herbs

Peel and slice eggplant. Sprinkle with salt and let stand for 30 minutes. Wash off salt and squeeze dry.
Fry in oil, adding onions and tomatoes. Arrange in layers with cheese in a casserole. Add water and seasonings. Bake 45 minutes in a moderate oven.

FOO FOO

5 green unpeeled bananas * water as needed
* salt and pepper to taste

(This is a well known African dumpling made with starchy foods such as green bananas, green plantains and sometimes mixed with cornmeal and seasoned. Here is a recipe from Barbados.)

Boil bananas, peel, then pound in a mortar. When fruit forms a paste, season with salt and pepper. Mould into balls and reheat in the oven, or drop into boiling water to reheat. Serves 4.

OKRA WITH TOMATOES

12 boiled okras 1 oz. flour
4 chopped tomatoes ½ pt. milk
4 tablespoons breadcrumbs * salt, pepper, thyme
1 oz. butter

Melt butter, stir in flour for 2 minutes. Remove from heat and add the milk gradually. Season and cook over low heat for 5 minutes.

Chop okras, mix with tomatoes and 2 tablespoons of the breadcrumbs. Turn into a baking dish and pour flour-milk mixture over this.

Sprinkle with remaining breadcrumbs and bake for about 15 minutes in a moderate oven.

PEAS AND RICE

1 cup red peas (soaked overnight) 1 sprig thyme
2 qrts. hot water 1 grated coconut
1 slice salt pork or beef 1 tablespoon oil
3 cups rice * a piece of hot pepper
* salt

Brown onion with salt pork and seasoning. Meanwhile, add 1 cup hot water to grated coconut and squeeze out cream.

Place peas in a pot with 2 quarts water and cook until tender. Add salt pork and seasonings and cook for ten minutes. Add rice and cook over low heat until ready. Add hot water if more liquid is needed.

STUFFED PAWPAW (PAPAYA)

1 green pawpaw (just streaked with yellow)
2 onions
2 cloves garlic
2 tomatoes
2 slices of ham or bacon
1 sweet pepper
1 hot pepper
1 tablespoon breadcrumbs
1 egg
* salt

Wash pawpaw. Cut off end and scoop out seeds. Chop onions, garlic, peppers and tomatoes and stew for 20 minutes.
Grill bacon and dice. Mix with breadcrumbs, egg and salt. Add to the vegetable stew and pack into pawpaw.
Cover with foil and set in a pan with a cup of water to bake in a moderate oven for an hour. Skin should not be eaten.

BAKED SWEET POTATO

Allow ½ potato per person
3 baked potatoes in skin
2 tablespoons grated coconut
3 tablespoons Red Stripe Beer
2 ozs. butter
* salt, cinnamon

• Cut potatoes in half, scoop out pulp. Crush with beer and butter. Add coconut and salt. Sprinkle with cinnamon and bake through to heat and serve.

PUMPKIN PUFF

2 cups hot mashed pumpkin
2 tablespoons butter
2 tablespoons minced onion
¼ cup milk
1 egg beaten
2 tablespoons flour
* a tip of baking powder
* salt, pepper

Heat oven to 400°. Combine all ingredients and bake in a casserole for 30 minutes.

YAM CASSEROLE

Yellow yam boiled and sliced
3 hard boiled eggs
½ cup grated cheese
1 cup white sauce
* salt, pepper

Place slices of yam alternately with sliced eggs and cheese in a casserole. Sprinkle with salt and pepper.
Make a white sauce and moisten yam mixture with 1 cup or more. Bake in a moderate oven till cheese is melted.

Salads

ACKEE SALAD

2 cups boiled ackees
2 chopped, hard boiled eggs
* a few strips of cooked chicken

Prepare ackees and boil for 1 minute. Turn into a colander and run cold water over the ackees, which must be firm.
Mix with chopped hard boiled eggs and strips of chicken. Season to taste.

AVOCADO AND GRAPEFRUIT

2 avocados
2 grapefruits
1 dessertspoon oil
1 dessertspoon vinegar
* salt to taste

Peel and remove seeds from avocados. Slice in circles. Place in individual plates. Fill centres with grapefruit segments. Cover with dressing of oil and vinegar.

BROAD BEAN SALAD

1 lb. broad beans (shelled)
½ lb. potatoes
2 hard boiled eggs
1 tablespoon diced sour pickles
* salt, pepper, oil and vinegar

Boil the beans in some salted water. Boil potatoes. Mix beans, diced potatoes, chopped eggs and pickles and season to taste. Moisten with oil and vinegar.

THREE-BEAN SALAD

- 1 cup cooked string beans
- 1 cup cooked red beans or peas
- 1 cup cooked broad beans
- ½ cup vinegar
- ¼ cup oil
- ½ onion finely chopped
- * chopped mint leaves
- * a pinch of sugar and salt

Mix beans together and toss with the last five ingredients.

STRING BEAN SALAD

- ½ lb. cooked beans
- 1 dessertspoon oil
- 1 dessertspoon vinegar
- ½ chopped onion
- * a few peanuts

Boil beans in salted water. Drain and dry in a cloth. Serve with oil and vinegar dressing and some chopped peanuts and onions.

BREADFRUIT SALAD

- 1 breadfruit
- 2 hardboiled eggs
- * mayonnaise, salt, pepper
- * a chopped shallot or small onion

Peel, dice, and boil breadfruit till just firm. Combine with eggs, shallot, salt and pepper. Moisten with mayonnaise.

CALLALOO SALAD

- 1 lb. callaloo or spinach
- 6 boiled, sliced potatoes
- 6 thin slices of cheese
- ½ cup mayonnaise
- * squeeze of lime juice

Plunge callaloo into boiling water for 3 minutes. Drain and chop.
Mix with cold sliced potatoes and thin slices of cheese. Dress with mayonnaise to which is added a squeeze of lime juice.

CARROT AND RAISIN SALAD

- 6 large carrots
- ½ cup raisins
- * oil and vinegar
- * lettuce or cabbage leaves

Shred carrots, mix with raisins and sprinkle with oil and vinegar. Serve on leaves.

CHICKEN SALAD

2 lbs. chicken	½ cup mayonnaise
2 cups diced pineapple	1 dessertspoon minced parsley
6 hard boiled eggs	* salt
1 cup green peas	

Boil chicken, remove the meat and chill. When chilled mix with pineapple, peas, salt and parsley, and toss with mayonnaise. Finally, crumble in the yolks and garnish with egg whites.

CHOCHO SALAD

3 chochos, peeled, sliced and boiled	* oil and vinegar
2 sliced onions	* salt and pepper

Place chochos in a shallow dish. Sprinkle with pepper, salt, oil and vinegar. Cover with sliced onions and some more of the oil and vinegar.

BAHAMIAN CONCH SALAD

12 young queen conch	¼ cup oil
3 hot peppers	2 sliced onions
½ cup vinegar	* salt
	* lime juice

Cover conch with water and bring to a boil, by which time it should be easy to remove the meat. Wash with lime juice and clean.

Dice and mix with chopped hot peppers, vinegar, oil, sliced onions and salt. This is a popular salad in the Bahamas.

CUCUMBER AND SOUR CREAM SALAD

1 cup sour cream	* a pinch of sugar
1 teaspoon vinegar	* sliced cucumbers
1 tablespoon chopped mint	

Mix together sour cream, vinegar, mint and sugar. Pour this over the sliced cucumbers. Marinate for an hour before serving.

JAMAICAN SALAD

1 cup freshly grated coconut
2 cups finely shredded cabbage
1 cup pineapple cubes

1 cup mayonnaise
* lettuce leaves

Combine coconut, cabbage and pineapple with mayonnaise mixing well. Chill and serve on lettuce leaves.

LOBSTER SALAD

1 cup mayonnaise
1 teaspoon onion powder
* lobster meat
* dressing

1 dessertspoon creole sauce
* shredded lettuce
* a few drops of lime juice

For each person arrange shredded lettuce on a plate. Top with a helping of lobster meat which has been tossed with the dressing below. Decorate with olives and strips of celery.

ONION SALAD

12 small onions
2 chopped tomatoes
* a handful of currants or raisins

* salt — parsley
* oil and vinegar to taste

Peel and boil onions in a small amount of salted water. When cooked add tomatoes, oil, vinegar, parsley and currants. Serve cold.

SWEET PEPPER SALAD

2 red sweet peppers
2 green sweet peppers

2 tablespoons oil
* oil and vinegar to taste

Cut and slice peppers. Take out veins and seeds. Saute quickly in oil. Drain. Add oil and vinegar with a pinch of salt.

POTATO SALAD

(A golden rule is that this must be made whilst potatoes are still hot).

- 6 boiled diced potatoes
- ½ diced onion
- 1 tablespoon flour
- 1 tablespoon vinegar
- 1 teaspoon sugar
- 1 tablespoon chopped parsley
- 6 boiled and sliced frankfurters (or vienna sausage)
- 2 tablespoons oil
- * salt, pepper

Fry frankfurters with onion in some oil. Add 1 tablespoon flour and blend. Add sugar, vinegar, parsley, salt and pepper. Mix together well and pour over the potatoes. Toss lightly.

PUMPKIN SALAD

- ½ pumpkin, peeled and boiled
- 1 teaspoon mixed herbs
- 1 tablespoon oil
- 1 dessertspoon vinegar
- * a few lettuce leaves

Place slices of firm boiled pumpkin on lettuce leaves. Make a dressing of herbs and oil and pour over pumpkin.

RICE OR MACARONI SALAD

- 2 cups cold cooked rice or macaroni
- 2 ozs. lean ham
- 4 stalks escallion
- 1 tomato
- 4 slices cucumber
- * herbs

Mix diced vegetables and rice with herbs and ham. Pour dressing over salad.

DRESSING
- 1 dessertspoon oil
- 1 dessertspoon vinegar
- 1 teaspoon soya sauce
- 1 teaspoon juice from mango chutney
- * a squeeze of lime — salt

Mix well together.

SHRIMP SALAD WITH COCONUT CREAM

1 cup milk
1 cup grated coconut
1 tablespoon oil
1 teaspoon salt
2 minced shallots

2 chopped sweet peppers
2 tablespoons soya sauce
1 tablespoon chopped peanuts
2 lbs. shrimp (cooked and peeled)

Combine milk and coconut in saucepan and bring to boil. Remove from heat and soak for 30 minutes. Press through a sieve to extract cream. Discard pulp.

Heat oil, and fry the shallots and peppers. Remove from heat. Add soya sauce and peanuts. Combine with coconut cream.

Arrange shrimps on a dish and pour dressing over them. Reserve a few shrimps for decoration and chill slightly to serve.

SALAD CREOLE

2/3 pineapple
1/3 of a tomato per person
½ cup fresh cream
1 tablespoon ketchup

* pinch of salt
* squeeze of lime juice
* chopped onion

Cut pineapple into thin strips and dice tomato. Combine next 4 ingredients and pour over salad. Serve on lettuce leaves and top with a sprinkle of chopped onions.

TROPICAL SALAD

1 cup grated coconut
1 cup diced pineapple

1 cup seeded tangerine segments
1 cup mayonnaise

Combine ingredients and serve on cabbage leaves or lettuce leaves.

Dressings & Sauces

COOKED SALAD DRESSING

- 2 ozs. butter
- 1 beaten egg
- ½ cup milk
- ¼ cup sugar
- 1 teaspoon dry mustard
- ¼ cup vinegar
- * pinch of salt

Melt butter. Add egg and milk and stir in sugar, salt and mustard, which have been blended with some vinegar.

Gradually add the rest of vinegar. Stir over low heat in a double boiler until thickened. Do not allow to boil. Cool and refrigerate.

HONEY DRESSING FOR FRUIT SALADS

- ½ cup vinegar
- 2 tablespoons honey
- ½ cup lime juice
- 3 tablespoons crushed pineapple

Mix together and chill.

A BASIC WHITE SAUCE

Melt 2 tablespoons margarine on low heat. Add ½ cup flour slowly, whilst stirring, with 1 cup of milk, and a pinch of salt until this thickens.
Do not allow to burn.

A HOT DRESSING

- ½ cup peanut butter
- ¼ cup tomato ketchup
- ¼ cup milk
- * a few drops hot sauce

Mix to a paste adding more milk if needed. Use over onions, cucumbers or sweet peppers.

OIL AND VINEGAR

¼ cup oil
1/6 cup vinegar

1 dessertspoon dry mustard
* pinch of salt

Mix well together.

MY SALAD DRESSING

¼ cup vinegar
2 teaspoons sugar

1 teaspoon mint jelly
* a squeeze of lime and a pinch of salt

Blend together and chill.

A DRESSING FOR SEA FOOD

4 tablespoons mayonnaise
4 tablespoons french dressing
2 tablespoons mango chutney

1 teaspoon lime juice
* a pinch of curry powder
* salt and pepper to taste

Combine and mix all ingredients.

SPICY DRESSING

3 tablespoons vinegar
2 tablespoons sugar

1 tablespoon powdered ginger

Blend together and chill. Delicious on crisp green salad.

---

2 MINUTE MAYONNAISE

1 teaspoon sugar
½ teaspoon salt
¼ teaspoon dry mustard

½ cup evaporated milk
½ cup oil
2 tablespoons vinegar

Mix all ingredients except oil and vinegar. Add oil gradually in a thin stream and beat well. Finally, add vinegar slowly, continuing to beat till smooth.

DEVILS SAUCE

- 2 tablespoons brown sugar
- 1 dessertspoon creole sauce
- 3 tablespoon ketchup
- ¼ teaspoon hot sauce
- 1 tablespoon guava jelly
- ¼ teaspoon salt
- 3 tablespoons vinegar

Mix all ingredients together in a saucepan and simmer for 2 minutes. Cool and chill.

EGG SAUCE

- ½ pt. evaporated milk
- 2 eggs
- 1 teaspoon vinegar
- 1 teaspoon lime juice
- ½ teaspoon pepper and salt

Hard boil eggs and chop. Mix with milk and other ingredients. Excellent over salads.

HOT PEPPER SAUCE

- 4 hot peppers
- 1 teaspoon oil
- 1 teaspoon creole sauce
- 1 teaspoon ketchup
- 1 teaspoon vinegar
- * salt to taste

Put peppers, and other ingredients through a blender or mincer. Bottle. Makes 1 bottle.

MARINA SAUCE

- ¼ cup oil
- 1 clove crushed garlic
- 2 teaspoons minced parsley
- 3 cups diced tomatoes
- 1 chopped sweet pepper
- * salt to taste

Mix well together and simmer slowly for 30 minutes. Cool and chill.

MARMALADE SAUCE

- 6 teaspoons dry mustard
- * marmalade to taste
- 2 teaspoons rum
- * soya sauce

Mix mustard with some rum to make a paste. Add marmalade and a few drops of soya sauce. Serve with barbecued dishes.

PEANUT SAUCE

2 cups crushed peanuts
1 tablespoon chopped onion
3 tomatoes
1 tablespoon fat

3 cups water
2 teaspoons curry powder
* salt

Put nuts into salted water and boil for 15 minutes. Fry onions and tomatoes and add to peanut mixture with curry powder. Simmer for about 20 minutes, stirring frequently.

PEPPERMINT SAUCE

2 egg whites
2 cups thin cream (evaporated milk)

1 tablespoon sugar
2 tablespoons creme de menthe

Beat egg whites stiff. Fold in cream, sugar and creme de menthe. Good over a fruit salad.

RUM SAUCE

4 ozs. butter
2 ozs. granulated sugar

2 tablespoons rum

Cream butter and sugar and add rum very slowly. Beat well and keep cool.

SABAYON SAUCE

4 ozs. sugar
2 tablespoons sherry

3 egg yolks
* few drops vanilla

Cream sugar and yolks together over a gentle heat. Add vanilla. Gradually add sherry and whisk vigorously until frothy and firm. Use immediately.

SWEET AND SOUR SAUCE

6 chopped shallots
2 tablespoons vinegar
1½ tablespoons brown sugar
½ teaspoon ketchup

1½ cups pineapple juice
1 teaspoon soya sauce
½ cup water
3 teaspoons cornstarch

Mix all ingredients except water and cornstarch and simmer gently for about 40 minutes. Mix cornstarch with water and add to the sauce. Simmer 5 minutes more, stirring until sauce thickens.

Caribbean Chosen Barbecues

BARBECUE COOKING CHART			
RARE	4 - 5 lb. Roast	2 - 2½ hours
MEDIUM	4 - 5 lb. Roast	2½ - 3 hours
WELL DONE	4 - 5 lb. Roast	3 - 4 hours

BACON-WRAPPED FRANKFURTERS

1 lb. frankfurters
4 ozs. cheddar cheese, sliced
8 rashers bacon
4 teaspoons mustard

Barbecue the frankfurters over medium coals for about 15 minutes, then slice them lengthways, almost through. Fill with cheese slices and press the frankfurters together again.

Spread the rashers of bacon with mustard and wrap around the frankfurters, securing the ends with wooden cocktail sticks. Place on the grill again and cook over medium coals for a further 5 minutes, or until cheese melts and bacon is crisp. Serve with a mixed green salad and potato chips.

Serves 4.

BAKED RED SNAPPER IN SAVOURY BARBECUE SAUCE

1 3 lb. red snapper
6 tablespoons butter
½ cup chopped onions
2 cups chopped celery
¼ cup chopped green peppers
3 cups canned tomatoes
1 tablespoon Worchestershire/ Pickapeppa sauce
1 tablespoon ketchup
1 teaspoon chili powder
½ lemon, finely sliced
1 teaspoon salt
2 bay leaves
2 teaspoons sugar
1 red pepper

Preheat oven to 350oF. Dredge snapper inside and out with seasoned flour. Place in baking pan. In a pot, melt butter. Add onions, celery and green peppers. Simmer until celery is tender. Add other remaining ingredients and simmer 15 minutes. Pour sauce over the fish. Bake approximately 45 minutes, basting frequently.

Serves 4—5 people.

BARBECUED CHICKEN

- 1 2½ lb. chicken, cut in serving pieces
- * black pepper
- * salt to taste
- * garlic

SAUCE
- ¼ cup chopped onions
- ½ cup water
- 2 tablespoons vinegar
- 1 tablespoon Worchestershire/ Pickapeppa sauce
- ¼ cup lemon juice
- 2 tablespoons sugar
- 1 cup chili/tomato sauce
- ¼ teaspoon paprika
- ½ teaspoon salt
- 1 teaspoon black pepper
- 1 teaspoon prepared mustard
- 1 teaspoon ketchup
- 1 tablespoon butter
- * hot pepper sauce to taste

Season chicken liberally with salt, black pepper, garlic. Let stand 1 hour.

To prepare sauce: Saute onions till brown. Add other sauce ingredients and simmer 15 minutes, then cool. Broil chicken. Add sauce when chicken is nearly done (after about 1 hour), basting continually. Serves 4.

BARBECUED CHICKEN WINGS

- 2 lbs. chicken wings
- 3 tablespoons honey
- 3 tablespoons vinegar
- 2 tablespoons sugar
- 3 tablespoons soy sauce
- 1 large clove garlic, crushed
- 1 stock cube
- ¼ pint hot water
- 1 tablespoon sherry

Cut and trim chicken wings. Place in a bowl. Blend together honey, vinegar, sugar, soy sauce and garlic, and pour over the meat. Dissolve stock cube in the hot water, then add the sherry. Add to the other ingredients in the bowl and stir together. Leave to marinade for 8 to 12 hours or overnight in the refrigerator. Preheat the oven to moderately slow at 335°F. Arrange chicken wings on a rack in a roast pan and baste well with the marinade. Bake, uncovered, until golden brown, basting occasionally with the sauce, turning once during the cooking time.

If served as a party-time snack, eat with fingers and provide a finger bowl of warm water and serviettes to wipe fingers.

BARBECUED CHICKEN WITH SPECIAL SAUCE

1   3 lb. chicken
1   cup tomato sauce or ketchup
1   teaspoon creole sauce
2   tablespoon vinegar
1   teaspoon dry mustard
1   teaspoon sugar
*   a drop or two of hot sauce

Cut chicken into pieces. Season with salt and pepper and grill over hot coals basting frequently with sauce made by combining last 6 ingredients and bringing them to a boil.

BARBECUED LAMB CHOPS

4   lbs. lamb chops
1   teaspoon prepared mustard
1   piece ginger, beaten
2   medium-sized onions, sliced
1   tablespoon salad oil
1   cup water
*   salt to taste
2   tablespoons chili/tomato sauce
1   tablespoon Worchestershire/ Pickapeppa sauce
1   tablespoon vinegar
*   hot pepper sauce to taste
*   black pepper

Season chops with mustard, ginger, salt and pepper. Place sliced onions over chops in baking pan. Combine other ingredients and pour over onions and chops. Bake, covered, in moderate oven, basting frequently, for approximately 15-20 minutes or until done. Remove lid 10 minutes before chops are cooked.
Serves 6.

BARBECUED MEAT BALLS

1 lb. ground beef
2 tablespoons chopped parsley
1 tablespoon bread crumbs
1 teaspoon salt
½ large onion
1 sprig thyme, chopped

1 egg yolk
1 tablespoon soft butter
1 teaspoon lemon juice
1 teaspoon black pepper
1 small sweet pepper
2 whole pimento grains

SAUCE
1 large sweet pepper
1 clove garlic
1 cup ketchup
1 teaspoon vinegar
1 piece ginger

1 large onion
1 carrot (cut up
 in long strips)
2 tablespoons sugar
½ teaspoon salt (to taste)

To prepare sauce: saute sweet pepper, onion, garlic, carrot in butter. Add other ingredients, then simmer for 20 minutes. Meanwhile, combine meatball ingredients, mold into balls. Skewer balls and place over flame, turning and basting continually with sauce.
Serves 4.

BARBECUED ORIENTAL CHICKEN

1 cup soy sauce
1 cup sake (Japanese rice wine) or
 1 cup grapefruit juice or 1 cup
 dry sherry
¼ cup cooking oil

1 teaspoon sugar
½ teaspoon grated fresh ginger root,
 or ground ginger
* one 2½ pound chicken, cut up

Mix together soy sauce, sake or grapefruit juice or sherry, sugar and ginger in a large shallow dish. Add chicken, turning to coat both sides. Cover and marinate in refrigerator, several hours or overnight, turning occasionally. Remove chicken from marinade and brush with oil. Grill about 6 inches from source of heat, brushing with marinade and turning frequently until brown and tender.
Serves 4.

BARBECUED PERCH

5 lb. perch
1 cup celery
1 cup onions
1 cup ketchup
1 tablespoon prepared mustard

1 tablespoon Worchestershire/
 Pickapeppa sauce
2 tablespoons vinegar
2 tablespoons sugar

Grill fish for 10 minutes. Meanwhile, sautee celery and onions. Combine other ingredients, bring to a boil. Baste fish with sauce, cooking for another 10 minutes.
Serves 6-8.

BARBECUED SPARERIBS (BAKED)

Please use the American style pork spareribs for this succulent recipe. If you can do the ribs over a good bed of charcoal, attending carefully to the basting, so much the better!

5 to 6 lb. spareribs cut in serving pieces	2 tablespoons lemon juice
1 lemon thinly sliced	1 teaspoon chili powder
¼ cup molasses	1 tablespoon celery seed
¼ cup prepared mustard	2 tablespoons Pickapeppa sauce
2 tablespoons vinegar	½ cup tomato ketchup
* salt to taste	

Place spareribs, meat side up, in a shallow pan. Sprinkle with salt. Top with lemon slices.

Bake in a moderate oven 350°F for 30 minutes.

Combine remaining ingredients and blend well. Remove lemon slices. Brush spareribs with mixture; turn and continue baking one hour longer, basting frequently.

Serve hot.

BARBECUED SPARE RIBS

2 lbs. spare ribs, cut in serving pieces	¼ oz. garlic powder
2 teaspoons salt	¼ oz. onion powder
4 pimento grains, crushed	½ cup paprika
* oregano	¼ cup lemon juice

SAUCE

¼ cup chopped onions	2 tablespoons brown sugar
1 tablespoon fat	½ cup chili/tomato sauce
½ cup water	½ teaspoon paprika
2 tablespoons vinegar	1 teaspoon black pepper
1 tablespoon Worchestershire/ Pickapeppa sauce	1 teaspoon prepared mustard
	* hot pepper sauce to taste

Season ribs with mixture of salt, oregano, garlic, onion and paprika. Rub in to meat well. Place ribs in moderate oven with a small amount of water, and cover. Cook for approximately ½ hour until almost tender. Remove from oven and cool. Place ribs on rack over coals, and turn continually until done (approximately 10 minutes). Make sauce by combining all ingredients and simmering for 10 minutes. Just a few minutes before removing from rack, brush ribs with sauce.

Serves 4.

BARBECUED STANDING RIBS (BEEF)

8 10 lbs. ribs
* salt
* black pepper
* garlic powder

SAUCE
14 ozs. ketchup
½ cup white vinegar
1 teaspoon sugar
1/8 teaspoon salt
½ teaspoon cumin
1 teaspoon coriander
1/8 teaspoon paprika
1/8 teaspoon saffron
¼ teaspoon ground ginger
1 red pepper, finely chopped

Season ribs liberally with salt, pepper, garlic powder; let stand overnight. When ready to cook, skewer beef, and cook over coals, turning very slowly, for about 2-3 hours. Meanwhile, combine sauce ingredients, simmer 15 minutes. Baste ribs with sauce only 15 minutes before removing from coals.
Serves 15 people.
To add an extra special touch, orange juice can be added to the basting mixture.

BARBECUED STEAK

2-2½ lbs. sirloin steak
8 ozs. olive oil
¼ cup soy sauce
* salt to taste
* black pepper
1 cup tomato sauce
2 tablespoons brown sugar
1 green pepper, cut in chunks
1 onion, sliced

Season steak with salt and pepper. Combine other ingredients, pour over steak. Marinate in refrigerator 4 hours or overnight, turning occasionally. Broil steak.
Serves 4.

BEEF LIVER IN BARBECUE SAUCE

1 lb. beef liver cut in ¼" slices
2 tablespoons butter or margarine
1 cup sliced onions
½ cup green sweet pepper, cut up
1 tablespoon vinegar
* salt and black pepper
1 tablespoon Pickapeppa sauce
1 teaspoon sugar
1 teaspoon prepared mustard
¼ cup tomato ketchup
½ teaspoon hot pepper sauce

Start heating oven to 325°F. Cut liver slices in half crosswise. Place half of slices side by side, in covered, shallow baking dish; sprinkle lightly with salt and pepper. Saute onion and sweet pepper in butter or margarine and arrange half on liver. Mix vinegar with next five ingredients with rest of liver then rest of sauce. Bake uncovered for 10 minutes.
Makes 4 servings. The family will need no encouragement to try this dish.

CHRISTMAS HAM WITH BARBECUE SAUCE

1 12-15 lbs. ham	2 tablespoons mustard
1 cup brown sugar	1 cup sherry

Preheat oven to 325°F. Bake ham, allowing 25 minutes per pound. When ham is almost done, remove from oven, score, and add cloves. Make a mixture of brown sugar and mustard, then add sherry. Mixture should be like a thick paste. Coat thickly over ham, then bake for another ½ hour.

JIFFY BARBECUE SAUCE

½ cup tomato ketchup
1 teaspoon dry mustard
1 teaspoon hot pepper sauce
2 teaspoons mango chutney

2 teaspoons Pickapeppa Sauce
* liquid from the can of corn & water to make ¾ cup

Combine all ingredients and pour over pork chops.

MEAT LOAF WITH BARBECUE SAUCE

LOAF
1½ lbs. ground beef
½ lb. ground lean pork
3 strips bacon, cut in small pieces
½ cup bread crumbs

½ cup tomato juice
2 eggs
2 tablespoons salt
2 tablespoons minced onions

GARNISH
8 bacon strips

* parsley sprigs

SAUCE
2 tablespoons ketchup
¼ teaspoon Worchestershire/ Pickapeppa sauce

¼ teaspoon chili powder
1 tablespoon minced onion
2 tablespoons vinegar

Combine all loaf ingredients. Shape into individual loaves (makes 8 loaves). Wrap a strip of bacon around each loaf. Simmer sauce ingredients for 15 minutes, then pour over loaves. Bake at 350°F for 45 minutes, basting once or twice during baking.

ORANGE GRILLED FISH

2 lbs. firm white fish

MARINADE
4 tablespoons soy sauce
2 tablespoons tomato ketchup
2 tablespoons chopped parsley

½ cup orange juice
* grated rind of ½ orange
* salt and blackpepper

Cut the fish into 1" pieces. Mix the ingredients for the marinade together, beating well. Pour over the fish and leave to marinate for 1 hour. Drain the fish and thread on six skewers. Grill over hot coals for about 8 minutes, then turn and grill for a further 7 minutes. Baste with the marinade during cooking.
Serves 6.

SHRIMP WITH COLD BARBECUE SAUCE

2 lbs. fresh shrimp
½ cup finely chopped celery
1 stalk skellion
6 tablespoons olive oil
3 tablespoons lemon juice
¼ cup ketchup
1 clove garlic

¼ teaspoon hot pepper sauce
5 tablespoons horseradish
2 tablespoons prepared mustard
¼ teaspoon paprika
¾ teaspoon salt
½ teaspoon white pepper

Clean then poach shrimp. To prepare sauce: rub bowl with garlic, then combine other ingredients. Marinate shrimp in sauce for an hour. Serve chilled on a bed of lettuce.

SMOKED PORK CHOPS, BAKED WITH JIFFY BARBECUE SAUCE

6 smoked pork chops
1 can whole kernel corn
1 egg, well beaten
1 cup chopped celery

1 onion, chopped
2 tablespoons oil
1 ounce margarine
1 green sweet pepper, chopped

Saute celery, onion and sweet green pepper in margarine, and mix with corn & egg. Brown chops lightly in oil, drain and arrange in a casserole. Cover with the corn mixture and pour sauce (see P 54) all over. Bake covered at 350°F for one hour. Remove cover during last 10 minutes.

SPICY ROAST BEEF BARBECUE

Roasted Irish potatoes, when done liberally drenched with butter or margarine, and maybe roasted ears of sweet corn, would be perfect accompaniments. To cool things off, how about a big cabbage slaw, dressed with Mayonnaise, sprinkled with paprika?

- 1 (4 - 5) Beef rump roast, rolled and tied
- ½ cup butter
- 1 cup vinegar
- ½ teaspoon dry mustard
- 1 tablespoon minced onion
- 1 tablespoon Pickapeppa Sauce
- ½ teaspoon Pimento
- ½ teaspoon coriander
- ¼ teaspoon chili powder
- 1 tablespoon lemon juice
- 1/3 cup brown sugar
- * salt and pepper to taste

Leave roast at room temperature for at least on hour. Start the fire in the barbecue, and let the charcoal bed burn until charcoal turns ash gray in colour. Tap the gray ash from the coals with fire tongs. After you start the fire, skewer the roast on the spit rod, through the centre of the roast. (If it is not centred properly, the spit will not turn.) Inset holding forks. When the fire is ready, start to brown the roast. While the roast is browning, combine the sauce ingredients in a saucepan, and heat until the butter melts. Makes about 2 cups. When roast is an even brown on all sides start to baste with the sauce, basting every 20 minutes until done.
(See Cooking Chart)

Pickles & Preserves

BREAD AND BUTTER PICKLES

1 qrt. sliced cucumbers
2 sliced onions
1 sliced green pepper
1 chopped clove garlic

1 cup sugar
½ teaspoon dry mustard
* pinch of salt
* vinegar and spices

Place onions, cucumbers, pepper, garlic and salt in a pan. Cover with ice cubes and let stand for 2 hours. Drain.

Combine other ingredients and pour over onion mixture. Heat to boil for a few minutes only. Seal while still hot in jars. Makes approx. 4 jars.

CORN RELISH

12 young corn ears
3 peppers (remove seeds)
1½ cups sugar
2 tablespoons salt

2 teaspoons flour
4 cups vinegar
4 onions
* mustard to taste

Remove corn from the cob. Put onions and pepper through a mincer and mix with corn. Cover with 3 cups of vinegar.

To remaining cup of vinegar add sugar, salt, flour and mustard to make a paste.

Add this to vegetable mixture and bring to a slow boil for 30 minutes.

Pour into hot jars and seal.

HOT PEPPERS AND SHALLOTS

6 hot peppers
2 cups white vinegar
* shallots to fill 2 jars
1 clove
* salt
* pimento grains

Slice peppers and remove seeds. Peel and wash shallots. Fill jars with shallots and hot pepper slices.

Boil vinegar with spices and salt. Pour over peppers and shallots and seal.

MANGO CHUTNEY

2 ozs. green ginger
2 lbs. brown sugar
1 lb. green mangoes — peel and slice
½ lb. raisins
1 tablespoon soya sauce
1 oz. garlic powder
2 ozs. salt
1 sliced hot pepper
1 sliced onion

Crush the ginger. Mix all ingredients and bring to a boil. Simmer gently until chutney is thick and syrupy. Correct seasoning.

RED DEVIL

6 peppers, seeded and diced
3 diced onions
1 pint vinegar
1 teaspoon nutmeg
* pinch of salt

Put hot peppers and onions through a mincer. Combine with vinegar, nutmeg and salt and bring to a boil.

Bottle when cool.

TO PRESERVE FRESH TOMATOES

Choose firm, ripe, small tomatoes without blemish. Put them into a jar with a large mouth. Fill jar with oil (corn oil preferably) so that tomatoes are covered with a layer of oil 1" deep. On top of oil pour a little brandy or rum and seal.

PICKLED WATERMELON

- 2 lbs. sugar
- 2 quarts water
- ¼ cup salt
- 1 pint vinegar
- * rind of watermelon
- 4 cloves
- 1 piece hot pepper
- * pieces of cinnamon stick (or grated nutmeg)

Peel off outer green skin of watermelon and chop the white flesh into pieces. Cover with water and salt and simmer until tender.

Bring remaining ingredients to a boil for 10 minutes. Add tender melon to this and continue to simmer until melon is transparent. Pack in jars. Approx. 4 jars.

VEGETABLE RELISH

- 6 carrots
- 1 pepper, seeds removed
- 2 onions
- 2 chochos
- 1 cucumber
- 6 olives
- 2 cups water

Chop carrots, peppers, onions, chochos, cucumbers and olives, add water to cover. Bring to a boil to tenderize. Drain.

DRESSING
- ½ cup oil
- 1 cup vinegar
- 2 tablespoon ketchup
- 1 tablespoon hot pepper sauce
- * salt to taste

Mix dressing and bring to a boil. Pour dressing over the vegetables, which have been packed in sterilized jars. Makes 4 jars.

GARLIC VINEGAR

Steep garlic cloves, which have been pricked with a pin, in vinegar for 10 days. Use for salad dressings.

HERB VINEGARS

Various herb vinegars can be made by loosely packing a jar with a combination of herbs and filling with vinegar.

Stand jar in a saucepan of water and bring to a boil slowly. Then allow to cool. After 2 weeks vinegar will be ready for use.

PEPPER WINE

Fill ¾ bottle with either cherry or bird peppers. Fill up with sherry or rum. Allow to stand for about one week before using.

Jellies & Jams

PINEAPPLE JAM

1 pineapple
* sugar
* nutmeg

Peel and grate the pineapple.
To each lb. of pineapple pulp, add ¾ lb. of sugar. Add nutmeg to taste.
Boil and stir until mixture thickens and sugar is melted. Seal in jars whilst hot. Makes approx. 3 jars.

PUMPKIN JAM

3 lbs. pumpkin
2 lbs. sugar
1 lime
1 orange
* salt

Peel and cut pumpkin into slices, then dice and pack in a jar. Add sugar.
Cover and stand for 12 hours. Drain off liquid and boil until syrupy. Add pumpkin, sliced lime and orange. Stir in a pinch of salt. Boil up, and cook until clear.
Seal in jars. Makes approx. 6 jars.

TOMATO JAM

8 tomatoes peeled and chopped
2 tablespoons lime juice
4 cups sugar
2 tablespoons chopped raisins
½ teaspoon all spice

Simmer tomatoes for 10 minutes. Add all ingredients except sugar and bring to a boil. Add sugar and continue to boil until sugar melts and mixture thickens. Skim and cool.

CALF'S FOOT JELLY

4 calves feet	2 cups sugar
5 qrts. cold water	1 pint sherry
* whites and crushed shells of eggs	½ teaspoon nutmeg
* juice of 3 limes	½ cup water
* juice of 1 orange	

Clean feet well and put into a pan of cold water. Bring slowly to a boil and simmer for 5 hours. Set aside to cool overnight. In the morning skim jelly from the top and discard sediment on bottom.

Put on heat and melt slowly. Add egg whites beaten to a froth, the crushed shells, nutmeg, sugar and fruit juices. Boil hard for 20 minutes without stirring.

Add 1 cup of water and let come to a boil again. Reduce heat and let simmer. covered for about 30 minutes.

Dip a flannel jelly bag into boiling water. Hang it up with a bowl underneath. Pour jelly into bag and let it drip. The bag must not be touched or jelly will cloud.

Turn jelly into a mould. Stir in wine and put in a cool place.

SEA GRAPE JELLY

7 lbs. sea grapes	* sugar
7 pints water	

Add grapes to water and bring to a boil. Stir with a wooden spoon and crush fruit whilst stirring. Boil about 20 minutes.

Drip through a sieve without stirring. Measure this juice and for every cup of liquid add an equal amount of sugar. Return sugar and liquid to heat and boil rapidly. Skim. Boil until a little tested on a plate will jell.

Pour into jars, and cool before sealing. Makes approx. 4-5 jars.

ORANGE JELLY
AND GUAVA JELLY

7 lbs. sliced guavas or 7 cups diced oranges	7 pints water (boil 30 minutes)
	* sugar

These are made to the same formula as seagrape jelly (see above).

Strain and measure juice in each instance, and add an equal amount of sugar. Boil until liquid jells — Pour into jars. Makes approx. 4-5 jars.

BLENDER GRAPEFRUIT MARMALADE

4 grapefruits	5 cups sugar
2 limes	1/8 teaspoon soda
1½ cups water	1 oz. gelatin powder

Lightly peel and seed grapefruit. Chop two and put into a blender with ½ cup water. Mince. Add soda to this and boil for 30 minutes.

Cut up remaining 2 grapefruits and limes discarding seeds. Add to ½ cup water and mince in blender. Add this to cooked mixture with rest of water and boil for 30 minutes.

Add sugar and stir and boil for 10-15 minutes, being careful to stir frequently to avoid burning and to melt sugar.

Add dissolved gelatin to marmalade when it has cooled slightly. Should make 4 jars.

ORANGE MARMALADE

4 large seville oranges	* sugar
2 teaspoons salt	

Wash oranges and peel lightly. Cut into quarters, removing pips and pulp. Cover pips and pulp with water and let stand overnight. Slice (or cut with scissors) the peel very thinly and add a little salt. Cover with water and soak overnight.

The next morning bring peel to a boil and boil until tender. Strain liquid from pips and pulp and add to the fruit mixture. Measure this and add sugar equal to this quantity.

Boil up again, simmer and stir until sugar melts and liquid thickens. Be careful not to burn, so at this point cook on a low flame.

When mixture jells, skim and remove and pour into jars.

GUAVA CHEESE

* ripe guavas (whatever number desired)	* sugar

Wash guavas, cut in half, cover with water and boil until tender. Rub through a sieve, weigh the pulp, and add an equal quantity of sugar.

Boil until mixture shrinks from sides of pot. Stir all the time to prevent burning.

When a little dropped into water forms a ball, pour into a shallow dish. Cool and cut into squares when firm.

LIME CURD

4 limes grated and juiced	4 ozs. butter
1 lb. granulated sugar	4 eggs. beaten

Combine all ingredients in a double boiler and simmer until sugar dissolves and mixture is thick. Makes 2 jars.

Desserts

AMBROSIA

4 oranges peeled and sliced
1 small shredded coconut
4 tablespoons wine
½ cup pomegranate seeds
* sugar

Pile fruit in alternate layers into a bowl, sprinkle with sugar, coconut and wine. End with a layer of pomegranate seeds.

BANANAS IN BATTER

3 ripe bananas
½ cup rum
1 tablespoon sugar
1 teaspoon lime juice
8 ozs. flour
* oil
1 oz. sugar
½ oz. butter
9 tablespoon milk
1 teaspoon baking powder
1 egg

Peel bananas and cut into thick chunks. Soak in rum, sugar and lime juice.
Mix remaining ingredients except the oil. Dip banana chunks into the batter using a perforated spoon. Fry lightly in hot oil.

RIPE BANANA PIE

2 sliced bananas
1 package lime jello — prepared as per instructions
* cherries
* shredded coconut (optional)

Place sliced bananas in a prebaked pie shell. Cover with cooked lime jello mixture. Chill.

BANANA PUDDING

6 ripe crushed bananas
3 tablespoons melted butter
1 glass white wine

½ lb. sugar
3 beaten egg white
* vanilla to taste

Mix all together and beat until smooth. Put into a souffle dish, and bake in a 325° oven until puffy and golden brown on top. Serve at once. The yolk may be used to make a sauce to serve with the pudding. Decorate with cherries and shredded coconut.

CASHEW NUT ICE CREAM

1 cup grape juice
½ cup chopped cashew nuts

1 qrt. vanilla ice cream
* pinch ginger powder

Mix the juice, nuts and ginger into the ice cream. Refreeze for about 2 hours.

COCONUT CREAM PIE

1½ cups milk
¾ cup grated coconut
3 eggs, separated
4 tablespoon sugar

1 teaspoon vanilla and a pinch of salt
2 cups flour
1 cup margarine
4 tablespoons ice water — salt to taste

Heat milk and set aside, beat yolks and add sugar, vanilla, salt and coconut. Stir in heated milk and fold in stiffly beaten egg whites.
Mix together flour, margarine, water and salt to form a dough. Roll out and line a pie dish. Prick the bottom. Pour in filling and bake for 50 minutes in a 350° oven.

COCONUT GIZZADAS

1 lb. brown sugar
¼ pt. water
1 grated coconut
½ teaspoon nutmeg

2 cups flour
¼ teaspoon salt
¼ cup margarine
* iced water to blend

Make a syrup of sugar and water. Add coconut and nutmeg. Mix well. Cool and fill pastry shells made as follows.
Mix flour and salt, cut in margarines and water. Roll out and cut into circles. Mould into cases and pinch up edges. Fill with mixture and bake in a 400° oven until pastry shells are golden brown.

COCONUT MOULD

1 tablespoon gelatin powder
¼ cup warm water

3 cups coconut cream
1 tin condensed milk

Dissolve gelatin in warm water. Mix with coconut cream and condensed milk. Heat through to melt gelatin, but do not boil or mixture will curdle. Cool and chill.

Per person
1 egg
1 oz. plain chocolate

1 tablespoon black coffee
1 tablespoon rum

Melt chocolate over low heat.
Separate eggs, reserving whites, beat yolks and stir into melted chocolate mixed with coffee and rum. Whip egg whites and fold into mixture.
Put into individual glasses and chill.

DUCKANOO

6 nearly dry corn on cob ears
1 cup brown sugar
1 dry coconut

½ cup raisins
2 tablespoons spice
* salt, ginger powder

Grate corn and coconut. Mix coconut with water to make 2 cups of cream. Add this liquid to remaining ingredients to make a paste.
Spoon into squares of banana leaf which have been dipped into boiling water briefly to make pliable. Tie into parcels.
Place in boiling water and steam for ¾ of an hour.

TROPICAL FRUIT SALAD

1 ripe pineapple or melon
* variety of diced fruits, as desired

* brandy, optional

Cut off the top of a ripe pineapple or use a melon cut into 2 parts. Scoop out flesh and mix with diced fruits — as many varieties as desired. Toss with 2 tablespoons brandy if desired.
Return to shell and chill. Fresh lychee and mangosteen can be added for a surprise. Both these fruit are obtainable in the Castleton area.

GUAVA MOUSSE

1 cup tinned guava nectar
1 tablespoon gelatin powder
2 tablespoons water
1 cup whipped cream

Dissolve gelatin in water and add to guava nectar. Heat slowly to melt gelatin. Cool slightly before adding the whipped cream. Set in individual glasses. Chill to serve.

GUAVA PIE

CRUST

1½ cups flour
2 tablespoons sugar
1¼ teaspoons baking powder
3 tablespoons butter
¾ cup milk
* a pinch of salt

Mix flour, sugar, baking powder and salt. Cut butter into this and blend until mixutre looks like cornmeal. Stir in milk.

Knead on a floured board for 1 minute. Divide dough into 2 balls. Roll out bottom crust, cut and fit into a greased pie dish. Put in filling of guava slices with some syrup.

Cover with remaining dough. Brush over with milk and make one or two slits in the pastry. Bake in a 350° oven for about 30 minutes.

FILLING

6 ripe guavas (when in season)
   or use tinned guavas
* water
* sugar

Peel fresh guavas, cut in half and scoop out seeds. Cover with water, add sugar and boil slowly until fruit is tender and a syrup has formed. Fill crust.

LIME PIE

2 egg yolks
4 ozs. condensed milk
¾ cup lime juice
* salt
6 tablespoons sugar
3 egg whites
1 baked pie shell

Beat yolks, stir in milk and add lime juice gradually. Beat well.

Whip egg whites with a pinch of salt and fold into mixture.

Pour into a baked pie shell and cover with meringue made with 3 stiffly beaten egg whites and 6 tablespoons sugar.

Bake in a preheated oven for 10 minutes — or until meringue is a golden colour.

MAMMEE APPLE PIE

1 mammee apple	1 cup water
1 8" baked pie shell	1 tablespoon lime juice
2 tablespoons brown sugar	½ teaspoon mixed spices

Make a syrup with sugar, water and lime juice.
Peel and scrape the fruit, slice and simmer gently in the syrup until tender. Fill the pre-baked crust and sprinkle with spices.
Chill and serve with cream — or coconut cream if desired.

PIE CRUST

8 ozs. flour	* pinch of salt
4 ozs. margarine	* cold water

Combine flour, margarine and salt. Add 2-3 tablespoons cold water to make a soft dough.
Roll out pastry larger than pie dish. Cut to fit, lapping over dish edge slightly. Cut a border and press it around the dampened edges of dish. Bake for ½ hour in 350° oven. Allow to cool before filling.

BOMBAY MANGO FOOL

6 Bombay mangoes	1 teaspoon lime juice
6 teaspoons condensed milk	* nutmeg
1 cup light cream	

Peel mangoes, slice flesh off seeds and put through a blender. Add milk, cream, lime juice and nutmeg. Stir well and chill.

BOMBAY MANGO SPECIAL

1 mango per person

Halve the mangoes and take out the seeds. Fill cavities with vanilla ice cream

NASEBERRY PANCAKES

1 cup milk
1 egg
1 egg yolk
1 tablespoon sugar

4 oz. flour
1 tablespoon butter
5 naseberries

Combine first 6 ingredients to make a batter. Add the naseberries, peeled and crushed. Mix well and drop by spoonfuls onto a hot, greased fry pan. Brown on both sides. Serve with butter or syrup.

ORANGE ICE BOX DESSERT

2 cups milk
2 tablespoons cornstarch
1 cup sugar
4 egg yolks
1 tabelspoon gelatin

2 tablespoons cold water
¾ cup orange juice
1 teaspoon orange rind
1 pt. whipped cream
* sponge cake slices

Heat milk in double boiler. Mix cornstarch, sugar and yolks and pour into warm milk. Cook slowly for 10 minutes.

Dissolve gelatin into warm water and add juice and rind. Place in refrigerator to chill and thicken.

Line a spring form pan with slices of sponge cake. Pour mixture over this and chill. Just before serving top with some whipped cream.

ORANGE SORBET

1½ pts. water
5 ozs. sugar
4 oranges

1 lime
1 glass white wine
1 egg white

Bring the sugar and water to a boil, dissolve and reduce.

Add the grated rind of 1 orange, and the juice of 4 oranges and 1 lime. Bring to a boil, strain and cool

Semi-freeze. Whisk egg white briskly and add along with wine to mixture. Freeze until mushy and serve in parfait glasses.

OTAHEITE PUDDING

ripe otaheite apples
¾ cup sugar
2 tablespoons butter or margarine

1 teaspoon spice
1 teaspoon baking powder

Peel and slice apples. Sprinkle sugar in a greased dish and dot with butter and spice. Arrange apple slices on top. Pour naseberry batter (see pg. 69) over the slices, or use other batter, adding 1 tsp. of baking powder. Bake at 350° for 35 minutes.

PICKNEY'S SWEET

½ jar of strawberry jam
* a little water

* whipped cream and chopped nuts

Heat jam with water to thin slightly. Pour into glasses. Cool and top with whipped cream and chopped nuts.

RUM COFFEE JELLY

2 tablespoons gelatin
2 cups of hot strong coffee
½ cup sugar
2 tablespoons lime juice

3 tablespoons rum
2 cups sour cream
1 cup brown sugar
½ teaspoon cinnamon

Soften gelatin in ½ cup of cold water. Add hot coffee and sugar and stir until gelatin is dissolved. Add lime juice and rum.

Pour into an 8" dish and chill until firm. Cut into cubes and serve a sauce made by beating together sour cream, sugar and cinnamon until sugar dissolves.

A TASTY, LOW-CHOLESTEROL RECIPE FOR PASTRY

1 cup flour
½ teaspoon salt
¼ cup vegetable oil

2 tablespoons skim milk (use instant) powder mixed in water

Mix flour and salt. Combine oil and milk and pour over flour. Stir with a fork till smooth. Shape into a ball, flatten and wrap with a sheet of waxed paper. Chill. Peel off the paper and roll out. Use as desired.

Cakes & Breads

BASIC BREAD DOUGH

2½ cups flour
1 teaspoon dry yeast
½ cup warm water
* pinch of salt

2 tablespoons melted butter
5 tablespoons cold milk
1 egg beaten into 1 tablespoon milk
2 tablespoons flour

Sift flour and salt. Dissolve yeast in ½ cup of warm water. Combine with butter and milk. Cover bowl and set aside to rise for 2 hours.

Put 2 tablespoons flour on table and pat dough to ½" thickness. Cut dough into 2 pieces and roll from corner to corner like a jelly roll.

Brush with egg and milk and slash surface at intervals. Place in bread loaf pans and bake 15 minutes in a fast oven, then lower to 350° and bake 15 minutes more.

BANANA BREAD

1 cup sugar
¼ cup margarine or butter
3 crushed, ripe bananas
2 cups flour

1 unbeaten egg
1 teaspoon baking powder
½ teaspoon soda
* vanilla flavouring

Cream sugar and butter. Add bananas and mix well. Add egg and dry ingredients and vanilla. Beat well.

Bake in a greased, paper lined loaf tin at 350° for 50 minutes. This freezes well.

EGG BREAD

1 pk. yeast	2 teaspoons sugar
4 cups flour	2 eggs (beaten)
1 cup warm water	1 egg yolk
1 tablespoon oil	

Soak yeast in warm water for 5 minutes. Sift flour, salt and sugar together. Add 1½ cups flour to the yeast and beat. Cover and allow to rise about 30 minutes.

Add the 2 eggs and remaining flour and oil to dough. Knead. Place in a bowl to rise for 2 hours.

Knead dough again. Divide into 3 strands and braid, turning ends under. Place on a greased sheet and let rise for 1 hour.

Preheat 400°. Brush the top with egg yolk. Bake for 10-15 minutes. Reduce oven to 350° and bake 30 minutes. Bread should be golden brown on top.

ORANGE BREAD

1 cup minced orange peel	1 cup milk
1 cup orange juice	½ teaspoon melted butter
2½ cups of sugar	2 teaspoons baking powder
1 beaten egg	* pinch of salt
3½ cups flour	

Combine orange peel and juice and boil until peel is tender. Add 1½ cups sugar, and boil slowly until thick and syrupy. Cool.

Mix egg, 1 cup sugar, butter and milk. Sift flour with baking powder and salt. Add mixture and stir. Add orange mixture to dough and blend well.

Pour into 2 loaf tins which have been greased and floured. Bake at 350° for 40 minutes. This is good toasted with cheese spread.

PUMPKIN BREAD

3 cups sugar	1 cup boiled, crushed pumpkin
1 cup oil	3 cups flour
4 eggs	

Grease and flour 2 loaf pans. Mix all ingredients together in a large bowl. Pour into pans.

Bake 1 hour at 350°. Cool for 10 minutes in the pan. Wrap in foil and store in the refrigerator.

SODA BREAD

1 lb. flour
1 cup warm milk

2 tablespoons soda
1 tablespoon salt

    Mix all ingredients and knead to a soft dough. Divide into 2 loaves.
    Brush with milk and dredge lightly with flour. Bake for 30-40 minutes or until lightly brown on top in a 425° oven.

BAKING POWDER BISCUITS

2 cups flour
2½ teaspoons baking powder
1/3 cup margarine

¾ cup milk
* salt

    Sift together flour and baking powder. Cut margarine into the flour mixture with a fork. Add milk and salt. Knead and roll out to ½" thickness.
    Cut into circles and bake on an ungreased sheet for 15 minutes in a hot oven, 400° - 450°.

BANANA MUFFINS

6½ ozs. flour
1 tablespoon corn flour
2 ozs. butter
3 ozs. sugar

1 egg
3 crushed bananas
1 teaspoon baking powder
½ teaspoon soda and a pinch of salt

    Sift together, flour, cornflour, baking powder, soda and salt. Cream butter and sugar. Beat egg and mix into creamed mixture.
    Add dry ingredients and crushed bananas alternately. Do not beat, but mix in well. Bake in greased muffin containers in 400° oven for 20 minutes.

BAPS

1 lb. flour
½ teaspoon salt
2 ozs. margarine

1 teaspoon sugar
½ pt. of warm milk
2 teaspoons yeast powder

    Rub margarine into flour and salt. Dissolve yeast in warm milk and add to the flour mix along with sugar.
    Allow to rise. Punch down, knead and divide into balls and roll out to an oval. Place on a sheet – dredge with flour and allow to rise again for 30 minutes – bake in a 400° oven.

BULLAS

3 cups flour	1 teaspoon baking powder
8 ozs. brown sugar	½ teaspoon soda
2 tablespoons melted butter	1 teaspoon nutmeg
2 ozs. water	½ teaspoon ginger powder

Make a syrup of water and sugar. Sift together dry ingredients and add syrup and melted butter.

Turn on to a floured board and pat into ¼" thickness. Cut into circles. Place on a greased tin and bake for 20 minutes in a 400° oven.

CASSAVA BAMMY

2 lbs. sweet cassavas

Scrape the cassava and grate. Squeeze out the juice, letting the flour remain. Rub through this flour to remove all lumps.

Put a thick-bottomed pan over a low heat and when hot, pour in the cassava flour. When it sets at the bottom, turn over and let the other side set. Scrape to remove any scorching.

Bammies may be moistened with a little milk and baked in a oven or browned under grill, or fry them in a pan with a little bacon fat. Each bammy should be about 5"-6" in diameter and about ½"-¾" thick.

CASSAVA PUFFS

1 lb. sweet cassava	1 teaspoon baking powder
1 tablespoon margarine	1 teaspoon salt
1 beaten egg	

Peel cassavas and boil until tender with some salt. Crush whilst still hot.

Add margarine, baking powder and beaten egg and beat.

Drop by spoonfuls into muffin tins which have been greased. Bake for 15 minutes in hot oven.

Puffs may also be fried.

A JAMAICAN BUN

1 lb. flour
2 ozs. butter
2 ozs. margarine
2 ozs. raisins
2 ozs. mixed peel
2 eggs

6 ozs. currants
½ lb. brown sugar
½ teaspoon nutmeg
½ teaspoon baking powder
* enough milk to make a batter

Blend butter and margarine into flour. Add baking powder, sugar and nutmeg. Add fruit to flour.
Beat the eggs and pour into the dry mixture adding enough milk to make a batter. Pour into a greased loaf tin and bake 1½ hours in a slow oven, about 300°.
Chopped cherries and some lime rind may be added to the mixture if desired.

COCONUT LOAF CAKE

½ cup butter
1½ cups sugar
2 + 2/3 cups flour
¾ cup milk

2 eggs
4 teaspoons baking powder
1 cup grated coconut
1 teaspoon vanilla

Cream butter and ½ of the sugar. Beat eggs with rest of sugar and combine the mixture.
Mix in flour and baking powder adding milk alternately with the dry ingredients. Add coconut and vanilla. Bake 1 hour in a 350° oven.

GUAVA LAYER CAKE

½ lb. margarine
1 cup sugar
2 eggs
2 cups flour
1 cup milk

2 teaspoons baking powder
¼ teaspoon nutmeg
½ teaspoon vanilla
* stewed guava slices, or use tinned

Cream margarine, sugar and eggs. Beat well. Add flour, baking powder and nutmeg. Pour in milk to which vanilla has been added.
Bake in two 9" layer tins for 30 minutes in a 350° oven. Cool and remove from pans. Spread guava slices between the layers. Sprinkle sugar lightly on top.
Stewed mangoes may be used in the same manner.

ORANGE CAKE

3 oranges
2 eggs
¾ cup sugar
2 cups flour

½ teaspoon soda and a tip of salt
1 cup butter
¼ cup grated orange rind

Squeeze juice from oranges to make 1 cup and reserve. Cream butter and sugar and add eggs one at a time, beating continuously.

Add flour, salt and soda, which have been sifted together. Continue to beat the mixture. Add ¼ cup of orange rind and the juice.

Pour into a greased 13" x 9" pan and bake in a moderate oven until firm.

RUM CAKE

½ cup butter
1 cup sugar
3 beaten eggs
¼ teaspoon salt
½ teaspoon baking powder
3 cups flour
* mixed spices

¼ cup milk
¼ cup molasses
2 cups peanuts (crushed)
1 lb. raisins
½ cup rum
* pinch of soda

Cream butter, sugar and eggs. Mix flour, baking powder, salt and spices. Add this to butter mixture and blend.

Add milk, soda and molasses, and add lastly crushed nuts, raisins and rum.

Bake in a loaf tin 300° for 2 hours.

KATIE'S SHORT BREAD

1 oz. sugar
4 ozs. butter

2½ ozs. flour
2½ ozs. cornflour (cornstarch)

Cream butter and sugar. Add flour and cornflour and blend thoroughly.

Put through a cookie tube or drop by spoonfuls onto a greased sheet. Bake for 10 minutes in a 375° oven. Sprinkle with sugar.

COCONUT COOKIES

¾ cup sugar
¼ lb. butter
1½ cups flour

1 tsp. baking powder
1½ cups grated coconut
1 beaten egg

Cream butter and sugar. Add flour and baking powder. Mix well then add grated coconut and egg.
Mix to a paste. Drop onto a greased cookie sheet by teaspoonfuls. Bake at 350° for 15 minutes. Makes approx. 2 doz.

GUAVA JELLY COOKIES

4 ozs. butter
2 ozs. sugar
1 egg yolk
½ teaspoon vanilla
4 ozs. flour

1 egg white
3 tablespoons chopped nuts
3 tablespoons guava jelly
* pinch of salt

Cream butter and sugar and beat in yolk and vanilla. Combine flour and salt and add to mixture.
Divide and shape into balls. Roll in egg white and then in nuts. Press a hole into each cookie and insert guava jelly.
Bake with jelly uppermost, on a sheet for 20 minutes in a moderate oven. Makes approx. 1 doz.

SWEET POTATO COOKIES

1½ cups flour
2 tablespoons brown sugar
4 teaspoons baking powder
5 tablespoons butter

1 cup crushed, boiled, sweet potato
½ cup of milk
* cinnamon

Combine all but milk and potatoes and mix until crumbly. Stir in crushed potatoes and milk.
Spoon batter on to a sheet.
Bake in a quick oven.
Split and serve with honey and butter. Makes approx. 1 doz.

Beverages

MATRIMONY

3 star apples
2 oranges

4 tablespoons condensed milk
* nutmeg

Remove starapple pulp. Peel orange and remove sections, discarding seeds.
Mix together, sweeten with condensed milk, and flavour with grated nutmeg. Chill.

NASEBERRY NECTAR

6 naseberries peeled and seeded
1 cup sugar

1 cup water
* juice of 1 orange

Put all ingredients through a blender, strain and serve chilled.

PLANATION RUM PUNCH

3 ozs. any rum
1 oz. lime juice

1 teaspoon honey
* nutmeg

Mix together and pour over cracked ice. Add a sprinkle of nutmeg.

SORREL APPETIZER

1 lb. prepared sorrel
2 ozs. grated green ginger
6 pints boiling water

Mix ingredients together, cover and leave overnight. Strain and add rum and sugar to taste. Serve over crushed ice.

SOURSOP PUNCH

1 ripe soursop
4 glasses water
* condensed milk to taste
* vanilla or rum to flavour

Peel and crush soursop, removing seeds. Stir in water and strain. Add milk and flavouring. Serve ice cold.

STARAPPLE APPETIZER

6 star apples (use pulp only)
2 tablespoons rum
2 tablespoons sugar
2 teaspoons lime juice
* angostura bitters

Cut star apples in half, remove pulp and mix with rum, sugar and lime juice. Add a few drops of angostura bitters. Serve chilled in fruit glasses.

For a full range of non-alcoholic beverages see CARIBBEAN COCKTAILS & MIXED DRINKS by Mike Henry

BANANA MILK-SHAKE

2 ripe bananas
1 pint milk (cold)
1 scoop vanilla ice cream
½ teaspoon vanilla

Puree the bananas in a blender. Add the cold milk, ice cream and vanilla. Blend well and serve in two tall glasses with straws. If the milk shake is very thick, it can be served over cracked ice.

CHRISTMAS CITRUS PUNCH

6 cups grapefruit juice
5 cups ortanique juice
3 cups orange juice
2 bottles soda water
¾ cup honey (or to taste)
1 whole orange, unpeeled
12 cloves

Stick the cloves into the orange and bake in a warm oven until hard.

Put the honey into a large bowl and add the fruit juices gradually, stirring so that the honey is completely dissolved. Add the baked orange. Allow the mixture to stand for two hours at least.

When ready to serve, place a block of ice in a large bowl and pour the punch over it. Use a ladle to pour the punch over the ice repeatedly until it is completely chilled. Add the soda water and serve.

Rum can be added to this punch while it is standing. It can also be garnished with sprigs of mint.

JAMAICAN GINGER BEER

¼ lb. root ginger
2 lbs. sugar
1 oz. yeast
1 lime
½ oz. cream of tartar
6 quarts boiling water

Grate ginger and place in a large bowl. Add the lime thinly sliced and cream of tartar. Pour the boiling water over all and allow to stand.

In a separate bowl, mix yeast with one cup sugar. Add ½ cup luke warm water to make a smooth paste.

When the ginger mixture is luke warm, add the yeast and sugar. Stir well. Cover. Let stand for 2-3 days. Skim and strain, then add the sugar, stirring well until it is dissolved. Pour into bottles and let the ginger beer stand at room temperature for three or four days more. Serve chilled. Rum can be added at the bottling stage, if desired.

Brunch

1. Hot Buttered Rum or Carrot Punch *
   Quickie Jerk Pork
   Solomon Gundy
   Banana Muffins
   Mango Fool

2. Boo Boo's Special *
   Curried Codfish
   Fruited Cabbage
   Baps
   Katie's Shortbread
   Coffee a la Mike

3. Policeman Glow *
   Ackee & Saltfish
   Stuffed Breadfruit
   Callaloo Salad
   Matrimony

4. Bloody Mary *
   Escoveitch of Fish (Grouper)
   Bammy
   Naseberry Pancakes served with syrup and butter, or orange jelly
   Jamaican Coffee

5. Coffee Coconut *
   Crab Fritters
   Cucumber and Sour Cream Salad garnished with sweet peppers
   Pumpkin Bread served with tomato jam
   Tropical Fruit Salad

6. Sour-Sop Punch *
   Liver with sweet pepper
   Cassava Puffs served with pineapple jam
   Ambrosia
   Coffee a la Blue Mountain

7. Naked Lady or Hot Barbados Rum Egg Nog*
   Fresh Fruit Plate
   Pepper Shrimps
   Ackee with Cheese
   Jamaican Bun

Lunch

1. Hot Flashes*
   Jamaica Fish Pie
   Pumpkin Salad garnished with sweet pepper rings and parsley
   Otaheite Pudding

2. Pineapple Cocktails*
   Jamaica Fish Tea
   Broad Bean Salad
   Beef & Mango in beer
   Yam Casserole
   Sliced Tomatoes
   Orange Sorbet

3. Air Conditioner*
   Jamaica Pepper Pot Soup
   Chicken Salad
   Sweet Pepper Salad
   Pumpkin Bread
   Coconut Mould

4. Banana Punch*
   Coco Soup
   Tropical Chicken   with rice
   String Bean Salad
   Rum Coffee Jelly

5. Woodpecker*
   Jamaican Salad
   Curried Goat with rice
   Mammee Apple Pie

6. Special Jamaican Rum Punch (hot) *
   Fish Chowder
   Poor Man's Fillet
   Rice & Peas
   Carrot & Raisin Salad
   Guava Mousse

7. Spanish Town *
   Pumpkin Soup
   Marinated Pork Chops
   Cho Cho Salad
   Breadfruit Salad
   Coconut Cream Pie

Dinner

1. Desperate Virgin *
   Grapefruit with shrimp & sour cream
   Jamaican Salad
   Conch Soup
   Salmi of Duck
   Pumpkin Puff
   Chochos baked with cheese
   Guava Layer Cake

2. Suffering Bastard *
   or Starapple Appetizer
   Avocado & Grapefruit Salad
   Gungo Pea Soup
   Pork Chops with Pineapple
   Baked Sweet Potatoes
   Coffee Mousse

3. Clarendon Cocktail *
   Ackee Salad
   Red Pea Soup
   Dumperpumpkin with rice
   Onion Salad
   Guava Pie

4. Frozen Daiquiri (Stella's Joy) *
   Lobster Salad
   Barbecued Lamb Chops
   Callaloo Bake
   Mint Glazed Carrots
   Orange Ice Box Dessert

5. Pineapple Caribbean *
   Conch Salad
   Barbecued Chicken
   Corn Fritters
   Cauliflower Custard
   Banana Pudding

6. Dry Martini *
   Shrimp Salad with coconut cream
   Cold Thick Cucumber Soup
   Boned Stuffed Leg of Kid with browned potatoes
   Egg Plant with Cheese & tomatoes
   Carrot Ambrosia
   Ripe banana pie

7. West Indian Punch *
   Tropical Salad
   Cho Cho Puree
   King Fish Fillets
   Yam Casserole
   Beans in sour cream sauce
   Lime Pie

---

* See Caribbean Cocktails by Mike Henry

GLOSSARY OF COOKING TERMS

Bain – Marie	A French cooking utensil similar to a double boiler used to cook over boiling water	Coat	To cover entire surface of food with flour, breadcrumbs, or batter
Bake	To cook by dry heat, usually in an oven	Cream	To combine butter or other shortening with sugar using a wooden spoon or mixer until light and fluffy
Barbecue	Generally refers to food cooked outdoors over an open fire with a spicy sauce	Croutons	Small cubes of fried bread
Baste	To brush or spoon liquid over food while cooking, to keep it moist	Cut in	To mix batter or margarine with dry ingredients, with pastry blender, knives or fork
Batter	Any combination which includes flour, milk, butter, eggs or the like for pancakes, coating, dipping etc.	Deep fry	To cook in deep hot fat or oil which covers the food until crisp and golden
Beat	To mix with a whisk beater or spoon so as to make the mixture smooth	Dice	To cut into small cubes
		Disjoint	To separate the joints – of poultry etc.
Blanch	To heat in boiling water or steam for a short period only to loosen skin, remove colour or set colour	Dot	To scatter small bits of butter or margarine over surface of food
		Flame	To spoon alcoholic fluid over and ignite, to warm the alcohol, and pour flaming over food
Blend	To mix two or more ingredients thoroughly		
Boil	To cook in any liquid at boiling point	Fold in	To use a spoon in a gentle rolling circular action as a means of combining ingredients
Bone	To remove bones from meat, poultry, game and fish		
Chill	To place in refrigerator until cold	Fry	To cook in hot fat using moderate to high heat

Ghee	Clarified butter, used in curries
Glaze	A thin coating of beaten egg-milk, syrup or aspic which is brushed over pastry, fruits, ham chicken etc.
Grate	To rub food against a grater to form small particles
Marinade	Liquid used for seasoning by soaking usually a mixture of oil, wine and seasonings
Marinate	To soak in a marinade to soften or add flavour
Parboil	To boil until partly cooked
Pate	A highly seasoned meat paste
Pit	To remove pit—stone or seed—from fruit
Poach	To cook gently in simmering liquid
Pound	To reduce to small particles or a paste, using a pestle and mortar
Preheat	To turn over to a selected temperature 10 minutes before it is needed
Grill	To cook by direct heat either over a charcoal fire or under a gas or electric grill unit
Julienne	A term for foods cut into thin strips like matches
Knead	To work dough with hands until it is of the desired elasticity or consistency
Puree	To press through a fine sieve or put through a food blender to produce a smooth mixture
Reduce	To cook over a high heat, uncovered until it is reduced to desired consistency
Roast	To cook meat by dry heat in the oven or on a spit
Roux	A mixture of fat and flour cooked slowly, stirring frequently — used to thicken sauces soups etc.
Salmi	A hash — usually of duck
Saute	To fry lightly in a small amount of fat turning and stirring frequently
Scald	To pour boiling water over foods, or bring to boiling.
Score	To cut narrow gashes on the surface of foods
Shred	To cut into fine strips
Simmer	To cook in liquid just below boiling point
Skim	To remove foam, fat or solid substances from the surface of a cooking mixture.
Sliver	To cut into long thin strips
Steam	To cook in vapour rising from boiling water
Stew	A long slow method of cooking in liquid in a covered pan, to tenderize tough meats.
Stir	To blend ingredients with a circular motion

Stock	A liquid containing the flavours, extracts, and nutrients of bones — meat — fish or vegetables, in which they are cooked	Toss	To mix lightly, using a fork and a spoon — i.e. salads chiefly
Toast	To brown in a toaster, or oven	Whip	To beat rapidly with hand or electric beater or wire whisk

---

35 USEFUL COOKING & HOUSEHOLD HINTS

1/3 to 1/2 teaspoon of dried herbs = 1 tablespoon fresh herbs.

Rub ½ lime on your hands or cutting board to remove onion, garlic or fish odours.

To avoid trouble with weevils, keep flour or cornmeal in a glass jar or plastic container in the refrigerator.

1 tablespoon oil in water for boiling pastas (macaroni etc.) prevents it from sticking together.

1 lb. coffee brews 40 cups.

For a tender pie crust use less water than is called for.

Dip knife in hot water to slice hard boiled eggs.

1 cup macaroni makes 2 cups of cooked macaroni.

Freeze left over coffee in an icecube tray. When used to chill iced coffee, the cubes will not dilute the coffee.

Parsley rinsed in hot water instead of cold retains more flavour.

Brown sugar will not become lumpy if stored in a jar with a piece of blotting paper fitted to the inside of the jar lid.

If food boils over in the oven, cover with salt to prevent smoking and excessive odour.

Add diced crisp bacon and a dash of nutmeg to cauliflower or cabbage for a gourmet touch.

To keep kettles clean, fill with cold water, add some ammonia and bring to a boil. Rinse well.

Gas ovens must be wiped clean before oven is cold. Racks and shelves must be washed with hot water and washing soda.

Wash pewter with hot water and soap, polish will scratch the surface.

Mildew stains can be removed by soaking overnight in sour milk. Dry in the sun without rinsing. Repeat process if necessary.

To remove a scorch, spread a paste of starch and cold water over the mark. Dry in sun and brush off.

Wash glass windows with crumpled newspaper dipped in cold water, to which has been added a few drops of ammonia.

For wood worms – apply kerosene oil with a brush to the infected area daily for 10 days.

To stop doors creaking rub hinges with soap.

Rust marks can be removed from steel by rubbing with a cut onion.

When washing thermos flasks, add a little vinegar to the water. It removes the musty smell. Do not cork flasks when storing.

To remove stains from china use a rag dipped in cold water and salt.

Before baking have ingredients at room temperature.

To chop sticky dried fruits, heat knife before using.

To prepare nuts, first blanch. Cover with cold water and bring to the boil. Let soak until skin wrinkles then slip the skin off between the fingers.

Parsley freezes well. Cut stems and place bunch in a plastic bag. Thaws easily.

Tear lettuce into pieces instead of cutting to prevent browning.

It is a good idea to make stock from left over bones and keep in the freezer to enhance soups and sauces.

Soak tarnished silver in hot water and ammonia – 1 tablespoon ammonia to 1 quart water.

Sour milk can be made by adding two teaspoons of lime juice to a cup of warm milk, which will curdle.

Moulds should be oiled before they are filled. Custards baked in hot water should be removed and left to stand for 5 minutes to settle before unmoulding. Run knife around the edge. Place a plate over the mould, invert the plate and mould and lift off.

As soon as vegetables are tender drain and plunge into cold water. This sets the colour. Vegetables may be stored and reheated when needed.

Whip cream in a large bowl set in ice. If no cream is available, place a tin of evaporated milk in the freezer for about one hour and then proceed to whip as for cream.
To sweeten, use icing sugar, which is preferable to granulated sugar.

TABLE OF MEASUREMENTS AND MISCELLANEOUS EQUIVALENTS

Dash	=	Less than 1/8 teaspoon
3 teaspoon	=	Tablespoon
4 tablespoons	=	¼ cup
8 tablespoons	=	½ cup
16 tablespoons	=	1 cup
1 cup	=	½ pint
2 cups	=	1 pint
4 cups	=	1 qrt.
2 liquid cups	=	1 lb.
2 pints	=	1 quart
4 quarts	=	1 gallon
1 fluid ounce	=	2 tablespoons
8 fluid ounces	=	1 cup
16 ounces	=	1 pound
1 lb. butter	=	2 cups
1 carrot	=	½ cup chopped
¼ lb. cheese	=	1 cup grated
1 envelope gelatin	=	1 tablespoon
1 teaspoon dried herbs	=	1 tablespoon fresh
juice of 1 lime	=	1 tablespoon
1 medium onion	=	¾ cup chopped
1 medium potato	=	½ cup chopped
1 pk. dry yeast	=	¼ oz.

SOME SUBSTITUTIONS

When you do not have exactly what the recipe calls for, here are some suggestions which are acceptable substitutes.

1 square cooking chocolate	3 tablespoons cocoa + 1 oz. butter
1 cup self raising flour	1 cup plain flour + 2 teaspoons of baking powder
1 cup sour milk	1 tablespoon lime juice or white vinegar + 1 cup milk
1 cup fresh milk	½ cup evaporated milk + ½ cup water
1 cup sour cream	1 cup warm milk + 1 tablespoon lime juice or white vinegar. Stirred to a thick consistency
Yeast compressed (1 oz.)	2 Teaspoons active dry yeast
1 fresh garlic clove	¼ teaspoon garlic powder
fresh green root ginger, grated	¼ – ½ teaspoon ground ginger

QUANTITIES PER HEAD

Appetizers	a variety of 4 - 6
Soup	5 servings to 1 quart
Sauces	10 servings to 1 pint
Fish	6 ozs. without bone
	8 ozs. with bone
Meat	4 ozs. without bone
	6 ozs. with bone
Green vegetables	6 servings 8 ozs.
Potatoes	4 servings 8 ozs.
Puddings/cold sweets	3 servings to 1 pint
Ices	10 servings to 1 quart
Poultry (chicken)	6 portions from a 4 lb. chicken
Poussin (chicken 3 - 4 weeks old)	i portion

USEFUL KITCHEN EQUIPMENT

Cake tester	Blender
Poultry shears	Food chopper
Colander	Meat pounder
Rotary egg whisk	Nut grinder
Pastry blender	Pots, pans, casseroles
Pastry brush	Knives
Cheese graters	Sieves, rubber scrapers, bulb basters

Pots must be heavy bottomed. The best all purpose material is undoubtedly heavy enamelled cast iron. Copper pots are very satisfactory — the metal should be 1/8" thick and the handle should be of iron. A kitchen should have round and oval casseroles. Saucepans in various sizes — a skillet (sloping sides) and a saute pan (straight sides).

Omelette Pan — This can be made of iron, with a long handle and a 2" sloping side and a 7" diameter bottom. This is perfect for 2 — 3 egg omelettes. When new, scrub with steel wool and scouring powder. Rinse and dry. Heat it and rub bottom with oil and let it stand overnight. Just before using, sprinkle 1 teaspoon of salt in the pan and rub with a paper towel.

Knives must be good quality, and kept in good condition. A 9" blade for chopping vegetables, a pointed knife for filleting, which should have a 6½" flexible blade. Knives for splitting chickens should have a 12" blade and should be heavy.

A carver should only be used for carving.

INDEX

A

Ackee & Salt Fish — see Salt Cod & Ackee	
Ackee Salad	37
Ackee Souffle	33
Ackee with Cheese	1
Ambrosia	63
Avocado & Grapefruit Salad	37

B

Baked Cabbage	31
Baked Black Crabs	12
Baked Grunts	14
Baked Spicy Snook	17
Baked Sweet Potato	36
Baking Powder Biscuits	72
Bald Pate Spatchcock	21
Banana King Fish with Mustard Sauce	12
Banana Bread	70
Banana Muffins	72
Banana Pudding	64
Bananas in Batter	63
Baps	72
Barbecues	
Bacon Wrapped Franks	47
Baked Red Snapper	47
Barbecued Chicken	48
Barbecued Chicken in Special Sauce	49
Barbecued Chicken Wings	48
Barbecued Lamb Chops	49
Barbecued Meat Balls	50
Barbecued Oriental Chicken	50
Barbecued Perch	50
Barbecued Spare Ribs	51
Barbecued Spare Ribs (Baked Style)	51
Barbecued Standing Ribs	52
Barbecued Steak	52
Beef Liver in Barbecue Sauce	52
Christmas Ham with Barbecue Sauce	53
Cooking Chart	49
Jiffy Barbecue Sauce	53
Meat Loaf with Barbecue Sauce	53
Orange Grilled Fish	54
Shrimp with Cold Barbecue Sauce	54
Smoked Pork Chops	54
Spicy Jiffy Beef Barbecue	55
Basic Bread Dough	70
Basic White Sauce	43
Beans in Sour Cream Sauce	30
Beef & Mango in Beer	24
Beef Curry with Green Bananas	24
Beef Soup	6
Beets with Orange Sauce	33
Biscuits — see Cakes & Breads	
Blender Grapefruit Marmalade	62
Bombay Mango Fool	67
Bombay Mango Special	67
Boned Stuffed Leg of Kid	26
Braised Duckling	22
Braised Guinea Hen	20
Brawn	28
Breads — See Cakes & Breads	
Bread & Butter Pickles	56
Breadfruit Salad	38
Broad Bean Cutlets	30
Broad Bean Salad	37
Bullas	73

C

Callaloo Bake	31
Callaloo Salad	38
Calf's Foot Jelly	61
Carrot Ambrosia	32
Carrot & Raisin Salad	38
Cashew Nut Ice Cream	64
Cassava Bammy	73
Cassava Puffs	73
Cauliflower Custard	32
Chicken Caymanas	18
Chicken Salad	39
Chicken with Lime & Olives	18
Christmas Citrus Punch	79
Cho Chos Baked with Cheese	32
Cho Cho Puree	6
Cho Cho Salad	39
Clear Turtle Soup	10
Cockerel Soup	7
Coco Fritters	3
Coco Soup	6
Coconut Chips	2
Coconut Cookies	76
Coconut Cream Pie	64
Coconut Gizzadas	64
Coconut Loaf Cake	74
Coconut Mould	65
Codfish Balls	12
Codfish Twice Laid	13
Coffee Mousse	65
Cold Thick Cucumber Soup	7
Conch Fritters	13
Conch Salad	39
Conch Soup	7
Cooked Dressing	43
Cookies — See Cakes & Breads	
Cooking & Household Hints	86
Corn Fritters	34
Corn Relish	56
Cow Heel Soup	7
Cow Peas Soup	8
Crab Fritters	13

Cucumber & Sour Cream Salad	39
Curried Goat or Rabbit	26

D

Devil's Sauce	45
Different Stuffing for Roasted Chicken	19
Dressing for Seafood	44
Drunk Chicken	18
Duck & Pineapple	23
Duckanoo	65
Dumperpumpkin	25

E

Egg Bread	71
Egg Plant Elegante	1
Egg Plant with Cheese & Tomatoes	34
Egg Sauce	45
Escoveitch of Fish	14

F

Fish Chowder	8
Food Substitutions	88
Foo Foo	35
Fried Plantain Chips	2
Fried Ackees	33
Fruited Cabbage	31
Fruity Callaloo	32

G

Garlic Vinegar	58
Glossary of Cooking Terms	84
Goat Head Soup	8
Grapefruit with Shrimp & Sour Cream	2
Guava Cheese	62
Guava Jelly	61
Guava Jelly Cookies	76
Guava Layer Cake	74
Guava Mousse	66
Guava Pie	66
Guinea Fowl Stew	20
Guinea Hen African Style	19
Gungo or Cow Peas Soup	8

H

Herb Vinegars	59
Honey Dressing for Fruit Salad	43
Hors D'oeuvres — See Appetizers & Hors D'oeuvres	
Hot Dressing	43
Hot Pepper Sauce	45
Hot Peppers & Shallots	57

I

Irish Moss — see Seaweed Soup	

J

Jamaica Fish Pie	14
Jamaica Fish Tea	8
Jamaica Ginger Beer	79
Jamaica Pepper Pot	9
Jamaica Salad	40
Jamaican Bun	74
Jams — see Jellies & Jams	
Jerk Pork Snacks	28

K

Katie's Short Bread	75
King Fish Fillets	15
King Fish in Coconut Cream	15
Kitchen Equipment	89

L

Lime Curd	62
Lime Pie	66
Liver with Sweet Peppers	27
Lobster Creole	15
Lobster Salad	40

M

Macaroni Salad	41
Mackerel Aloha	15
Mammee Apple Pie	67
Mango Chutney	57
Mango Fool	67
Marinated Pork Chops	27
Marine Sauce	45
Marmalade Sauce	45
Matrimony	77
Menus	
Brunch	80
Lunch	81
Dinner	82
Mint Glazed Carrots	32
Mutton Stew	26
My Salad Dressing	44

N

Naseberry Nectar	77
Naseberry Pancakes	68

O

Octopus	16
Oil & Vinegar Dressing	44
Okra with Tomatoes	35
Onion Salad	40
Orange Bread	71
Orange Cake	75
Orange Ice Box Dessert	68
Orange Jelly	61
Orange Marmalade	62
Orange Sorbet	68
Otaheiti Pudding	69
Oysters	3

P

Pata Cake	3
Paw Paw Soup	9
Peanut Sauce	46
Peppermint Sauce	46
Pepper Shrimps	3
Pepper Wine	59
Pickled Watermelon	58
Pickney's Sweet	78
Pigeon Pie	20
Pigeons with Cabbage	21
Pigeons with Pineapple	21
Pineapple Appetizer	2
Pineapple Jam	60
Plantation Rum Punch	77
Poor Man's Fillet	26
Pork Chops with Ginger Ale	27
Pork Chops with Pineapple	27
Pork Rind	2
Potato Salad	41
Preserves — see Pickles & Preserves	
Pumpkin Bread	71
Pumpkin Jam	60
Pumpkin Puff	36
Pumpkin Salad	41
Pumpkin Soup	9

Q

Quantities Per Head	89

R

Rabbit Fricassee	28
Red Devil	57
Red Pea Soup	10
Red Stripe Batter for Fish	17
Rice & Peas	35
Rice or Macaroni Salad	41
Rio Cobre Mud	4
Ripe Banana Pie	63
Roasted Rabbit	29
Rum Cake	75
Rum Coffee Jelly	69
Rum Sauce	46
Rump Steak Casserole	25

S

Sabayan Sauce	46
Salad Creole	42
Salmi of Duck	22
Salt Cod & Ackee	13
Salted Beef & Banana Casserole	24
Sauces — see Dressings & Sauces	
Sea Grape Jelly	61
Sea Urchin	4
Sea Weed Soup	9
Seasoned Breadfruit Chips	5
Shellfish — see Fish & Shellfish	
Shrimp Salad with Coconut Cream	42
Shrimp with Pineapple	16
Soda Bread	72
Solomon Gundy	17
Sorrel Appetizer	78
Soursop Punch	78
Souse	29
Spicy Dressing	44
Stamp & Go	11
Starapple Appetizer	78
String Bean Salad	38
Stuffed Breadfruit	31
Stuffed Calepeeva	11
Stuffed Cho Cho	34
Stuffed Paw Paw	36
Stuffed Squash	34
Sweet & Sour Sauce	46
Sweet Pepper Salad	40
Sweet Potato Cookies	76

T

Table of Measurements	88
Tasty Low Cholestrol Recipe for Pastry	69
Tasty Jerk Pork Bites	5
Teal with Orange Sauce	23
Thick Turtle Soup	10
Three Bean Salad	38
Tomato Jam	60
To Preserve Fresh Tomatoes	57
Tripe Soup	10
Tripe Windsor	29
Tropical Chicken	19
Tropical Fruit Salad	65
Tropical Salad	42
Two Minute Mayonnaise	44

V

Vegetable Relish	58

W

Watermelon Marbles	4
White Wing	22

Y

Yam Casserole	36